MOVE
UPSTREAM

MOVE UPSTREAM

A Call to Solve Overpopulation

KAREN I. SHRAGG

Minneapolis–St. Paul

Library of Congress Control Number: 2015948097

Cover and interior design by Robaire Ream

ISBN: 9780988493834

To my dear friend
and colleague Ed Levering

Table of Contents

Author's Note

> Once it was necessary that the people should multiply and be fruitful if the race was to survive. But now to preserve the race it is necessary that the people hold back the power of propagation.
>
> —Helen Keller

This book has been in progress for over five years. During that time it became even clearer to me how important and timely this topic is because I had to keep changing the population numbers from just under 7 billion to 7.2 billion. As soon as this is published, those numbers will unfortunately become obsolete too.

Throughout this book I cite examples of organizations and individuals to more clearly illustrate the ways many groups and public figures are failing to address this crisis. I have selected the groups that are well known and provide the best illustration for my arguments. There are literally thousands of other groups and individuals who are similarly glossing over this issue that could have just as easily been featured.

Of the 12 books I have written, this was by far the most challenging. It wasn't difficult because of the topic; it was difficult because the people I am pushing to do more are people who are already doing so much. The activists I take on in this book continue to be people I admire very much. It is my hope that they will feel that I am in their court.

The world certainly doesn't need any more books with scary forecasts. What it does need is a book on how *not* to waste our activism on projects that have no hope of being successful *if* we do not meet the challenge of overpopulation head on.

The people I highlight in this book are still my heroes, even if they are misguided and uninformed when it comes to deeply understanding the one issue that could help them the most. No issue is exempt from the truth that we must live within the laws of physics. As Canadian biologist David Suzuki frequently reminds us, Homo sapiens must obey the laws that govern the earth. Our biosphere is a closed system and we have been breaking its laws for a long time. We are already suffering from our transgressions and this will worsen over time. We need to wake up, educate, organize and take action on an issue that holds the key to success. In this book I demonstrate how overpopulation is preventing long-term success on so many of the issues we care about, and what we can do about it.

Karen I. Shragg
September 2015

Chapter 1

Obeying Nature's Laws

Either we decide to manage our own numbers,
to avoid a collision course . . . or nature will do
it for us in the form of famines, thirst, climate
chaos, crashing ecosystems opportunistic
disease and wars.

—Alan Weisman

If you are a person who reads the first and last lines of a book to see what it is about, I am beginning and ending this book with the same sentiment: Overpopulation is our biggest, most ignored problem on Planet Earth and it is solvable. The solutions are compassionate because we will be volunteering to have fewer children in order to prevent a catastrophic ending to life as we know it. There are two sides to the issues we are facing due to the overconsumption of the vital and limited resources on our planet: the individual acts of consumption and the amount of actual consumers. We have focused most of our attention on the struggle to increase our resources through conservation and technology while our numbers have been spinning out of control. It is time to eliminate the taboo of talking about the human numbers side of the equation. We can no longer afford to continue to think that even talk of overpopulation is somehow draconian. I will spend much of this book addressing the many parties who must wake up in order to make the compassionate solutions before us become reality.

I teach my students that humans are a part of the animal world. As such, we need to obey its laws just like other animals do. This grounds students in a reality they often miss. I tell my students that they have only three choices: They can be classified as plants, animals or minerals. "We're *not* animals, we're people," is their frequent reply.

Not long ago, a student compromised with, "We're manamals!" They are not alone in this perception.

We treat this planet as if humans are an exception. Ignoring nature's rules and her boundaries is commonplace. We don't see the fallout from our actions and typically blame multi-national corporations and government agencies as the source of all of our environmental problems. While they are certainly guilty of crimes against the environment, our sheer numbers alone put us in resource overshoot every day. "Overshoot" is the term for using up resources faster than they can be replaced. There are over 7 billion of us. We are growing by 1 million every 4.5 days. This pressure is creating irreplaceable resource deficits which must be addressed if we truly want to make a difference.

People frequently act as if we are exempt from the rules of carrying capacity. Carrying capacity is the number of organisms that a region can support without environmental degradation year after year.

Every animal has limits set by its habits and habitat. An average-sized white-tail deer eats 8–10 pounds of tree buds a day during the winter months. Too many deer in a given habitat will alter the forest and ultimately result in starving deer when the forest is over-browsed.

The Canada goose is another great example. I manage a nature center in Minnesota and have witnessed these otherwise beautiful birds becoming so numerous they are often hated. Their droppings commonly litter trails, beaches and golf courses. While they themselves are temporarily thriving, they are clearly impacting their environment and if not controlled will run out of resources at some point.

It is easy to tell when an animal exceeds the carrying capacity of its habitat. The area suffers degradation and is unable to support plants and animals up and down its food chain. Nature becomes out of balance. When looking in the mirror, we must begin seeing a species that has exceeded its carrying capacity. We are a bipedal hominid with a large brain, which makes us extraordinarily adept at altering our environment as we see fit. Our ingenuity often has the negative side effect of draining limited resources. Because we are so overpopulated, we have to be careful to watch out for the fallout every time we invent something to increase our comfort and enjoyment. When we develop a taste for a new drink or food and it becomes popular we are in danger of stretching our resources too thin.

The popularity of sushi has helped endanger bluefin tuna, which is favored by sushi chefs. Due to the demand for sushi in the best restaurants, bluefin are now being caught faster than they can reproduce and are threatened with extinction. Their status is driven by overpopulation and they are listed on the Monterey Bay Aquarium's

Seafood Watch List as a fish to avoid. No plant or animal is immune from disaster if it has the misfortune of becoming popular for food, fashion or functional use. The exotic pet trade is exacerbated by over-population too.

We live on a planet suffering from the effects of global overshoot. The Global Footprint Network defines global overshoot as occurring:

> . . . when humanity's demand on nature exceeds the biosphere's supply, or regenerative capacity. Such overshoot leads to a deple-tion of Earth's life supporting natural capital and a buildup of waste. At the global level, ecological deficit and overshoot are the same, since there is no net-import of resources to the planet. Local overshoot occurs when a local ecosystem is exploited more rapidly than it can renew itself.

There are many ways to measure overshoot scientifically, but the anecdotal evidence is compelling. We have degraded habitats, polluted waters, depleted fisheries, forced thousands of animal extinctions and destabilized global climate by adding more carbon to the atmosphere than it can handle. Our daily lives often include increased traffic, ever bigger crowds, and longer lines. Countries further along on this deadly journey experience famines. We have collectively turned a blind eye to this reality. In our efforts to cure diseases, decrease infant mortal-ity and infertility, we have increased our longevity and our ability to reproduce. We focus research and development dollars on increasing the comfort of the already privileged. Every monster-sized television screen, talking smart phone, slick vehicle and kitchen device requires non-renewable resources. This pressure ultimately destroys the en-vironment, endangers wildlife and puts the future of our species in jeopardy.

Though rarely discussed, overpopulation is clearly a problem in the United States. Alan Kuper, the late founder and president of Comprehensive U.S. Sustainable Population, said,

> The American public is not demanding government action to achieve reduced consumption, greater efficiency in energy use, or reductions in population. The media sometimes present con-servation in a favorable light, but the idea of gradually reducing the U.S. population seldom receives attention, unless it is pre-sented as a threat to the economy. Almost never do the media portray reduction in human numbers as a beneficial step away from the impossibility of endless population growth. As popula-tion and consumption grow, stocks of nonrenewable resources

dwindle. Obviously this cannot continue. Since change is inevitable, the public should be informed of the possible benefits of a gradual transition to long-term sustainability.

I think it is very important to focus the conversation on the positive effects of smaller populations. Kuper lists the following benefits of achieving a significantly smaller U.S. population: "[F]ull employment, more direct democracy, a cleaner, healthier environment with fewer costly environmental problems, less congestion, crowding, and sprawl, more stable communities and institutions, more set-asides of natural areas for wildlife habitat and recreation, fewer costly military interventions overseas to secure access to foreign resources."

Pulitzer Prize winning author Alice Walker said, "Activism is the rent I pay for living on this planet." I define activists as people who devote their lives, or at least their spare time, to making the world a better place. These honorable individuals range from food shelf volunteers to those marching in the streets to protest the latest war. I strongly urge activists everywhere to help break the silence on the overpopulation issue. We are already far exceeding the earth's capacity to sustain us. This book is unique in that I focus on the fact that overpopulation is solvable. Any solution must start with a full understanding and discussion of the issue. It cannot be solved in silence.

Most activism is focused downstream. Downstream acts focus on symptoms. Upstream acts focus on the causes of problems. The approach taken to solving present problems is often like reaching for cough syrup to cure a smoker's cough.

Activists who ignore the realities of overpopulation in their discourse will perpetually struggle downstream. They think failure to succeed is based on a lack of funds or political will, when breaking nature's rules is the true cause.

The task of improving the environment is frequently put on each individual. We are all told to reduce, reuse and recycle, but humanely reducing family size is not a part of the message. The website Liveecologically.com defines sustainability as "living in a way that does not put a heavy demand on the environment and resources." There is no way that we can live sustainably with unchecked population growth on our limited planet. Very few environmental groups have websites which recommend smaller families as a part of living sustainably on the planet. Most ignore the impact of our swelling numbers on depleting resources.

In the following chapters, I cite examples of how well-intentioned activists are making things worse by ignoring the realities of carrying capacity. It is difficult to criticize activists who are popular heroes because they could just as easily spend their time and resources increasing their own wealth and buying more luxuries. My main premise is that activists can only be truly successful in their own missions if they move upstream by including the overpopulation issue. They need to help us awaken the world to the fact that humans are subject to the laws of carrying capacity, just like deer, geese and all other species. The Food and Agriculture Organization of the United Nations predicts that by 2025, 1.8 billion people will be living in countries or regions with absolute water scarcity. We cannot solve these desperate problems with technology alone.

I became an activist in the tenth grade at Golden Valley High School in Minnesota. Mr. Kimbal, my social studies teacher, encouraged us to strike our school and door knock to raise awareness about the illegal invasion of Cambodia by American forces. He taught us that we were each responsible to make the world a better place, even if it meant breaking the rules. That same year I read Paul Ehrlich's iconic book *The Population Bomb*, sealing my fate as an overpopulation activist.

I have taken a few detours, thinking I could make a difference in other ways. As vice president of a national peace organization I helped develop Peace Pole sites. To protect local wildlife areas I became a board member of a wilderness preserve and an Izaac Walton chapter. I became a vegan and an organic gardener, gave speeches on saving rainforest, attended many national Earth Day protests and countless anti-war protests. I devoted decades to teaching environmental education and have been a guest speaker at many naturalist conferences. I still do many of those things, but now I couple them with this upstream issue. It is overwhelming to realize that in the course my career, approximately 2 billion people have been added to the planet. No wonder it feels like so little progress has been made.

Working upstream means trying to get humans to live within our planet's ecological limits. It is more socially acceptable to discuss how each person can reduce consumption than it is to have a conversation about reduction in human numbers. Encouraging people to use a cloth bag is easier than dealing with education about condom use. Meanwhile we must keep reminding ourselves that we add one million passengers to our planet every 4.5 days. We cannot let political correctness get in the way of doing the right thing. Steven Geske, author of *Healing Leadership: A Survival Guide for the Enlightened Leader*, writes that, "It won't matter how many parking lot barriers are made out of milk cartons if our planet becomes uninhabitable. We must start caring about our very own carrying capacity numbers and act accordingly."

In chapter three I will delve deeper into the data that support the claim that we are overpopulated. What is important to know is that it is easier now than ever to measure our remaining vital resources and how fast we are growing. Global Footprint Network is one of the organizations that keeps track of these numbers. Their best estimate is that a sustainable number of humans for the planet is about two billion. This assumes people will be living a more European lifestyle, with smaller homes and fewer cars. If we want to live like Americans with big homes, cars and boats, that number is much less.

My target audience for this book is very bright people who care deeply about our planet, but dismiss overpopulation. All too frequently environmental activists work on downstream issues. Overpopulation creates tangible problems in its wake that require a lot of time and attention. One could spend an entire lifetime working just on pollution or water scarcity. The point of my book is that unless and until we also work to bring about sustainable population numbers, these displacement issues will not get resolved.

One of the biggest myths about overpopulation is that people often assume it is a problem exclusively for developing nations. Every country has limited resources and the U.S. is no exception. No one can live without water. California's drought has serious and worldwide implications. The drought crisis has created a buzz around water conservation as in government restriction of personal water use, climate change and changes in agricultural practices. The news has not focused much attention at all on the fact that California is the most populous state in the nation. In 1900 it had 2 million residents. In 2050 the projected population of this state is 50 million. Claiming that the U.S. is exempt from overpopulation because we are a modern country is a statement of denial and ignorance. Each of our watersheds can easily become overpopulated because we cannot continue to take more water out of the ground than can be replenished by water cycles. In California satellite measurements show that the aquifers of the Sacramento and the San Joaqin River basins were being overdrafted (pumping higher than the rate of recharge) by 12,000,000 acre feet of water per year between the years 2011 and 2014. The Ogalala aquifer is located in the Great Plains roughly between Nebraska and Texas. It is not set up to recharge. We depend on it to irrigate our croplands which feed us and the world and yet this water will not be there forever. It is draining fast.

Activist Lester Brown said, "The world has set in motion environmental trends that are threatening civilization itself. We are crossing environmental thresholds and violating deadlines set by nature." I particularly like his last line, "Nature is the timekeeper, but we cannot see the clock." I believe that most of us are choosing not to see the clock because we think that it is easier.

I hope to awaken activists to the realities of carrying capacity and invite them to move upstream where their efforts are much more viable. I hope this book will clearly show that it is our responsibility as environmental leaders and progressives to tell the whole truth and never again be satisfied by working exclusively on displacement issues. By creating a path that includes the reality of overpopulation, we can join hands and pursue a progressive path together. We can and we must achieve our mutual goals of leaving resources and opportunities intact for future generations and reducing misery and suffering in the world.

Chapter 2

Science Says
Paying Attention to Cues and Data

The hungry world cannot be fed until and unless
the growth of its resources and the growth of
its population come into balance. Each man
and each woman and each nation must make
decisions of conscience and policy in the face of
this great problem.

—Lyndon B. Johnson.

Volumes of well-researched data have been collected about how we are overwhelming our finite resources with our numbers. *Scarcity* by Chris Clugston warns us about the way we are quickly running out of the 89 non-renewable metals, fuels and substances our society relies on to power our society. *Overshoot: The Ecological Basis for Revolutionary Change* by William R. Catton Jr. warns that we are already in overshoot with no hope to make gains with renewable technology. *Man Swarm and the Killing of Wildlife* by David Foreman points out how over-population is dooming many wild species to extinction. *Countdown* by Alan Weisman illustrates the situation regarding population in the 21 countries he studied.

While they all have done impeccable and indisputable research about how fast we are running out of resources, they do not strongly promote the notion that overpopulation is solvable. It is important to restate some of their facts in order to remove any doubt that this issue is very real and currently upon us. It is also important to open our eyes to see that every day, in every country of the world we are being affected by overpopulation. Whether we have crowded cities or are having our resources extracted due to overpopulation pressure, this is a very real issue we are experiencing all around the U.S. and the world today.

I was once in a traffic jam near Fort Meyers, Florida, with some friends. The conversation went something like this. "It must be a Twins' spring training game." "No, it must be construction." When it turned out to be neither of those, the next suggestion was that it must have been an accident. There was no accident. As we were crawling along the freeway at a snail's pace in the middle of the week I quickly called my friend at World Population Balance. "What is the population of Florida?" I asked. He responded that it was 19 million and growing by 250,000 every two years. By comparison, Iowa is about the same square miles and has four million people in it. When my group arrived at our destination I told them that we had just experienced overpopulation. It had never occurred to them that that was even a possibility. I pointed out that there are too many people using too few resources. In this case, the freeways could not accommodate demand in a way that was efficient.

The Twin Cities of Minnesota is where I was born and have lived most of my life. There was a highway that was under construction for four miserable years with the promise that traffic would flow much more smoothly once the Department of Transportation project was completed. Now that Highway 62 is straighter it is more crowded than ever, because during those four years that traffic kept increasing due to a growing population. Millions were spent and the result could never be as promised due to overpopulation. North Dakota is experiencing an oil boom complete with its problems. They now have higher crime, more pollution and more arrests for DWIs. These problems can also be blamed on overpopulation. Too many people nationally and globally demanding finite oil have created the right economic climate for extracting dirty oil. There are countless examples like these. What is important is that we recognize what is behind it all.

In my talks on this subject I ask the audience to imagine that they are in charge of a country about the size of Wisconsin. They have endless power, access to technology and billions of dollars to give each and every person a high quality of life. The only problem is that this country is already filled with 156.6 million people. The question is, can you remedy this situation with money, power and technology? This is not a fictitious country. This country is Bangladesh. In 1973 ex-Beatle George Harrison wanted to help this beleaguered war torn and storm hit country so he held a concert. The concert raised a quarter of a million dollars back when it only had 67 million people living there. The proceeds from CD sales continued and the concert proceeds exceeded 12 million dollars. I bet they wish they had spent it on birth control and education because Bangladesh is virtually a failed state. Without a serious plan to curb births, they will be unable to stop the hemorrhaging of a country overrun with too many people.

We are now all on the spectrum belonging to failed states. Every day we ignore this issue we inch and crawl closer to being more and more like Bangladesh every day. If a country is not working to reduce their numbers they are doomed to continuing to ask for aid for their poverty stricken people.

If you know someone who is 80 years old, something astounding happened in their lifetime. The world added a destabilizing unsustainable 5 billion people to its population. In one person's lifetime the world grew by a number we can barely comprehend. My father was born in 1926, the year before the world reached two billion people. The earth could have sustained the 2 billion, but not the additional 5 billion added in my father's lifetime. In geological time this growth happened with lightning speed.

There is some debate about what would be a sustainable number of humans because it depends on what lifestyle and what resources are currently available. Some say as few as 100 million, others say as many as 3 billion. At any rate, it is billions below our current 7.2 billion. Consumption rates vary greatly between countries, but still each human has the same minimum needs. Even though a person in the U.S. consumes 17 times more resources than a person in India, we all need water, food, shelter and energy to power our lives. Ideally, each of us in this overcrowded world would like a quality of life which includes food, work, energy, water and healthcare security. While it is conceivable that we could solve one of these problems through technology, the rest of these needs would still make us unsustainable. If we were to solve the energy crisis with a breakthrough in solar technology, we still won't have enough soil to grow our food or water for everyone. Figure out how to hydroponically grow our food supply and we still have a crisis for finding enough water and the rest of the resources we need in a modern world. Add to the mix that we are growing by 73 million people a year and it's a real mess of failing to play catch up.

The facts of our current state of population verses vital resources are both sobering and overwhelming. It is easy to see why we are in collective denial about them because frankly it is very depressing. Few want to hear about how quickly we are running out of the very building blocks of life as we know it. However, the premise of this book is that we cannot solve what we do not confront. So here goes:

- In 2014 the world population reached 7.2 billion.
- Sustainable global population is between 1.5 and 3 billion depending on the lifestyle at which people live.
- US sustainable population is approximately 150 million and in 2015 population was already at 320 million.
- While it is true the rate of growth has slowed from about 93 million to 73 million, that isn't much to celebrate in a world that is already using up so many non-renewable resources.
- Our species has *doubled* in the past 45 years.
- The Earth's population is increasing by over 140 people every minute. This is equivalent to adding another Los Angeles plus another Chicago to our limited planet every month.
- Modern humans demand a lot of room and resources. Multiply individual needs for food, water, energy, and shelter by billions and here's what happens:

  - We are driving over 50 species of plants and animals to extinction per day!
  - We are destroying rain forests many times faster than they can regenerate.
  - We are consuming stored solar energy (fossil fuels) at rates thousands of times faster than it is regenerating.
  - We are consuming fresh water at least 10 times faster than it is being replenished in regions of northern Africa, the Middle East, India, Pakistan, China, and the U.S.
  - We are causing soil salinization and erosion several-fold faster than rates of restoration.
  - We are over-fishing our oceans, radically changing the species balance in many places.

- For several years population has been increasing faster than many vital non-renewable and renewable resources. This means the amount of these resources per person is declining, in spite of modern technology. Using up resources faster than they can be replaced is called "overshoot" and is referred to many times in the chapters that follow.
- Other massive social and environmental problems, such as political instability, loss of freedoms, vanishing species, rain forest destruction, desertification, garbage, urban sprawl, water shortages, traffic jams, toxic waste, oil spills, air and water pollution,

increasing violence and crime, all continue to worsen as our numbers increase by more than 70 million more people every year. Solving these problems will be much less difficult when we stop increasing the number of people affected by them.

- Two billion people live in poverty, more than the population of the entire planet less than 100 years ago.
- Today there are more people suffering in misery and starvation in the world than ever before in history.

Chapter 3

Moving It All Upstream

Of all the interconnected problems we face,
perhaps the most serious is the proliferation of
our own species.

—Sir Crispin Tickell

Matt Damon is doing it. Sean Penn is doing it. Bill Clinton is doing it too. What are they are doing? They are selflessly trying to improve the dire living conditions of people around the world.

These famous, wealthy and powerful people volunteer their time and money with the intention of reducing misery and suffering. Their intentions deserve our applause. They eschew selfishness and share their influence trying to make the world a better place.

While they are busy fighting the ravages of malnutrition, lack of potable water, disease and poverty, the hurdle of overpopulation is holding them back. The symptoms they and many others like them fight are the unavoidable results of local populations exceeding the capacity of their water, soil and energy resources. To successfully reduce suffering, groups like Water.org must also work on stabilizing and reducing populations while trying to bring clean water to them.

Numbers can be misleading. A 1.2% annual growth rate on our planet doesn't sound like much but that represents an extra 81 million people on an already struggling planet. Locally, that growth is represented unevenly across the planet. One example of an overpopulation hotspot is Nigeria. From 1990 to 2010 Nigeria's population grew by 62%. In only twenty years it added 60,861,000 people to a country with fixed boundaries. Non-profits keep trying to solve this overpopulation crisis with foreign aid. Helping people out of misery today can have the unintended consequence of contributing to overpopulation tomorrow. Distributing food to countries on the brink of collapse helps perpetuate unsustainable numbers if equal efforts to stabilize and reduce births and population are not implemented.

Our civilization is based on limited fossil fuels and minerals. The faster these resources are used, the faster they are disappearing for good. It is ironic that overpopulation has sentenced all countries to live under the burden of decreasing and irreplaceable vital natural resources in a global economy. Overpopulation must be solved both at the local and global level. In 2008 I gave a talk about the problems of overpopulation to officials in Belize. This Central American country had a fairly stable population due to a brain drain of its college-ready citizens seeking to be educated out of the country. Neighboring Guatemala does have an overpopulation problem. People in Guatemala look to Belize as an overpopulation release valve. As they come across the border Belizeans will experience a rise in population and subsequent poverty as more people overwhelm their resources. Immigration most frequently flows from countries which are overpopulated to those which are soon to be overpopulated.

Many of the developing countries are simply further along on the journey towards scarcity. In the U.S. we are over-pumping our aquifers, but there is still water in them. Overpopulated Sub-Saharan Africa, on the other hand, is under chronic water stress, with only 22 to 34 percent of the people having access to safe water.

According to Global Footprint Network, "Today, humanity uses the equivalent of 1.5 planets to provide the resources we use and absorb our waste. This means it now takes the Earth one year and six months to regenerate what we use in a year."

We are experiencing overshoot today with a growing population of 7.2 billion people. This means that resources will continue on their downward slide as the population increases even if we are all suddenly inspired to drive electric cars, live in green homes and become vegetarians.

Evidence of overpopulation in the U.S. may not be as obvious as in the developing world but it still exists in measurable ways. The Ogallala, or High Plains aquifer, which covers a vast area from Nebraska to Texas, is being pumped much faster that it can be replenished. It formed ten million years ago and is the largest aquifer in the world at 174,000 square kilometers. Due to erosion and lack of glaciers it is no longer replenished with water from the Rockies. This is the world's largest known aquifer with an approximate area of 174,000 square miles. This is not sustainable. Ancient aquifer water is being used to irrigate crops and golf courses, fill pools and bathtubs, and this precious water will dry up unless we can reduce population. Present day shortages of water and other resources illustrate that the U.S. is overpopulated relative to its resource base even though vast open spaces exist in the American West. Open space is not the issue. The issue is the inability of vital natural resources to continue to supply civilization at current and rising rates of consumption.

Aligning demand and resources is key to addressing the issues activists care about. It is the missing piece to success. We cannot reduce suffering in the world *only* by getting smarter about distribution and technology. What possible technology could neutralize the demand put on resources by our numbers? Remember that one million people are added net gain to the earth every 4.5 days. Everyone needs to memorize this statistic. Population growth and overpopulation put the brakes on progress. They sidetrack success. They override every attempt to reduce misery and suffering in the long run.

We must recognize that we shot past the opportunity to stabilize our population at a sustainable level of 2 billion about 80 years ago. We must now focus on humanely reducing population on the planet. Some recognize this harsh truth, but most are focused on symptoms. The issue of overpopulation is feared, ignored, misunderstood, falsely represented and demonized by people from all political and religious persuasions. The concept of too many people using up the earth's limited resources lies outside the parameters of the typical activist's world. It flies in the face of current norms and doesn't fit into society's dominant anthropocentric worldview.

A concept called "scotoma" may also be in play. Scotoma means blind spot and can be physical as well as metaphorical. A metaphorical scotoma is the inability to see or understand what is obvious to others. My grandfather, of blessed memory, had a scotoma about space flight. He was born in 1895 and just could not believe that Neil Armstrong actually walked on the moon. He would shake his head at the television set and tell us he believed that it was all filmed in Hollywood.

Metaphorical scotomas are actually quite common. The modern incarnation of The Flat Earth Society began in 1956 and still exists, its members claiming that the photos of the earth as a sphere are a part of a vast conspiracy. Some people become infected with metaphorical scotomas because they are deeply concerned about one issue which clouds all others. Many who are vehemently anti-abortion have unfortunately conflated that issue with overpopulation. Their worldview is that anything that could be remotely connected to abortion must be wrong. These frightened and myopic groups claim that overpopulation is a myth in true scotomatic fashion.

Labeling this phenomenon has helped me understand why people repeatedly fail to see overpopulation as a motivating factor of destruction on our planet. It is right in front of them but they cannot see overpopulation as a driving force of resource destruction. They have no direct context for it. Our societal narrative worships growth and the promotion of human welfare. The truth about overpopulation is too hard to grasp in this context. Cultural noise drowns out the reality of resource depletion created by the over-demand of too many people living on a limited planet.

Activists of all types typically focus on relieving suffering, not on its causes. It reminds me of the time a doctor treated my knee pain with a bandage, never looking at the pronation in my foot for the actual source of my problem.

Urgent issues permeate each moment of our lives. The challenge is to strive to see what is causing all the problems. To achieve long-term success, activists must incorporate the message of humane reduction of human numbers in all attempts to better the world.

Without interviewing each of the people mentioned in this book, it is impossible to know their precise feelings about overpopulation. They may be completely unaware, in denial or may feel it is best to do what they can and leave the challenges of overpopulation to population groups. Perhaps they will let me know some day. I ask them to imagine the great things that could be accomplished if we paid attention to both human numbers *and* efficient use of resources. Imagine the possibilities if they made the overpopulation connection to their issues.

When it comes to the overpopulation issue, there are deniers of various stripes. Like the climate change deniers, they fight the issue either overtly or by omission. Overpopulation deniers range from those who may intellectually agree but never work on the issue to those who actively oppose it.

Activists who are overpopulation deniers address problems without addressing the cause. They focus on displacement issues caused by overpopulation. They navigate the world on a micro scale, too busy or distracted to learn the connection between overpopulation and their cause. They do not realize that so many of their issues are negatively impacted by overpopulation.

Some deniers spend their time and energy developing arguments that re-write population as insignificant compared with what can be done on the consumption side of the equation. They contend that our numbers don't really matter because we are going to farm fish, increase grain yields, create rain gardens and make recycled plastic furniture. They look at population predictions from years ago that have been revised downward and believe that success on the issue is being achieved. Some deniers go so far as to call overpopulation activists racists. Without really understanding the issue, they look at them and say that they are most often white people who want people of color to stop reproducing.

Other deniers know about this issue on some level and agree it is problematic, but opt out of educating people about our unsustainable numbers. Those who dodge this issue often share with me that they feel it is hopeless. I completely understand why they focus their energies on building birdhouses or ladders for spawning salmon. These are all tangible things to do even though it will not be an adequate response in the long run. I know people who have attended workshops on overpopulation but refuse to get involved in any substantial way. They become overwhelmed with how tough this issue can be and settle on helping with some downstream goal at their favorite charity.

The Ethiopian famine of the mid-1980s inspired the song "We Are the World" produced by Quincy Jones. This popular song raised millions of dollars to help desperate people in their time of need. However, no funds were provided to help the Ethiopians from continuing to expand their population. Ethiopia's population has climbed from 42 million in the 1980s to over 83 million today. Ethiopians are once again on the verge of another overpopulation-inspired disaster due to this doubling. Their country is susceptible to drought and has poor sanitation which means their natural resource base of soil and water cannot support the people struggling to live there. Sending money to build better sanitation will not work without curbing and reducing population. One can only hope that the next fundraising song includes lyrics encouraging small families.

Rotary International is well known for its displacement issue projects at home and abroad. Rotarians are dedicated people, but I believe they cannot achieve truly successful missions while ignoring the devastating effects of overpopulation. Many people I know are Rotarians. They typically choose a country that is suffering and get busy fixing things. They build schools, dig deeper wells, vaccinate and bring in much needed food and clothing. Kind and passionate philanthropists, they bring smiles to children who instantly love them for building schools and providing basic needs. The people Rotarians help today will grow into adults who will reproduce in unsustainable numbers tomorrow. Their noble efforts will be undermined without a comprehensive family planning education and birth control program in place that will result in a population decline.

Obstacles for Rotarians and others are not just within their groups. Many countries live under age-old religious doctrines and cultural norms which affect their population numbers. Often, male dominated cultures view a large family size as a sign of prowess. Others will continue to have children until they have males because females require costly dowries and will not provide for their elderly parents. Although these patterns are hard to break, Bill Ryerson of Population Media Center has had some remarkable success developing culturally respectful soap operas and radio dramas to help change people's attitudes about family size in countries all over the world.

Approximately 10,000 years ago modern agriculture replaced the hunter-gatherer system of previous human existence. This was revolutionary for it permitted populations to grow beyond their limits. Food scarcity had been the limiting factor for hunter gatherers. When modern agriculture produces a surplus of food, we naturally get a surplus of people to go along with it. Similarly, when we intervene with humanitarian projects and provide food for the starving and undernourished we permit more life to happen in places unable to sustain their populations. It is critical that activists around the world and at home work upstream when offering humanitarian aid. Aid should always be accompanied with birth control. Otherwise larger famines will keep occurring.

The Bill and Melinda Gates Foundation recognizes the value of investing in voluntary family planning. They do very commendable work trying to break down the cultural, monetary and physical barriers that prevent access to birth control to an estimated 220 million women in developing countries. However, one is hard pressed to see a reference to overpopulation on the Foundation's website. Preventing unwanted pregnancies is mentioned, but no statement is made that the countries they work in are already overpopulated relative to their resource base. The Gates Foundation states that they want to improve women's lives but their lives cannot improve for very long in overpopulated areas. Overpopulation prevents a good quality of life for anyone struggling to live where resources are stressed.

I don't want to understate that the Bill and Melinda Gates Foundation does critically important work, but they need to take the next step and name overpopulation as a source of the problem.

They will never reach their goals because there is not a global context for their work. Overpopulation needs to be named and understood so that comprehensive policies and programs will be put into place. We must set up a world that favors fewer of us. This will take informed, empowered, well-educated women and men who grasp the blunt truth about overpopulation.

Women struggle for many rights all across our planet. Focusing our limited resources solely on women's empowerment will not achieve enough traction in time. We have to clearly see the degradation already being driven by overpopulation so it can be tackled humanely with every resource we possess. We cannot relegate solving this upstream problem to the hopeful result of women's empowerment. It cannot simply be an afterthought of working on women's issues. It must be much more comprehensive and deeply rooted.

Those with deep pockets and big hearts often operate without realizing how overpopulated we are relative to our resource base. Overpopulation is either completely lost on celebrities or they are too afraid to deal with it in public.

Many celebrities have more than two children but devote a lot of time to saving the world. It is representative of a lack of understanding that saving the world must include recognizing the role overpopulation plays in the problems we are trying to solve. The longer we delay action, the less desirable our options become. First, we must swallow the hard pill of science. We are already swimming in a deep well of overpopulation. Stabilizing world population at over 7 billion will NOT be enough. That keeps us in overshoot. Intellectuals squabble over where our population will stabilize, if at all. Whether it is at 9 billion or 11 billion won't really matter. Stabilizing at ANY of those numbers is simply settling for a different speed of resource collapse and total disaster.

People often ask me if it would work to return to the Stop at Two mantra, which was made popular around the world in the 1970s. The answer would be yes *if* we only had a growth problem. Stopping growth used to be the answer, but now we have an *over*population problem. Reducing only our growth each year on the planet is not the whole solution anymore.

We are having the wrong debate. The debate must be about how to give humanity a clear, humane and sobering message that this is a solvable issue with means available and at a relatively low cost. *One Child Families Can Save Humanity* is the message that reflects what we need to say today. "Stop at two" is outdated because we have kicked this can down the road for too long. That would keep us at the unsustainable number of 7.2 billion. We cannot pretend that doing anything downstream will do enough to help in the long run unless we also advocate for a humane global effort to reduce overpopulation.

Chapter 4

Conservationists in Denial

> I have often thought that at the end of the day,
> we would have saved more wildlife if we had
> spent all WWF's money on buying condoms.
>
> —Sir Peter Scott

Sir Peter Scott was right. The fight to save individual species has won some battles but overall we are losing the war. Long-term conservation efforts will lose out if conservationists do not partner with overpopulation activists to save wildlife.

The wildlife conservation story is two-pronged. One part says habitat must be protected with fences, guards and laws. The other says, "Teach people to care about wildlife and they will take care of it." This story could only work long-term in a world with a population stabilized at a sustainable level.

My heart is with the efforts of conservation organizations to save lions, whales, polar bears, spotted leopards and a long list of wildlife species. Unfortunately, they pursue these efforts without telling the whole story. Most nature programs I watch on television contain a message which goes something like this, "The flying fox fruit bats of Australia are running out of habitat so they are coming into the cities to eat from fruit trees". Or the commentator says, "The popularity of sushi is causing many species to collapse." Rarely do these programs tell the complete story that overpopulation is driving these problems.

It is only slightly encouraging to see World Wildlife Fund state on its website that:

> Humanity's annual demand on the natural world has exceeded what the Earth can renew in a year since the 1970s. This "ecological overshoot" has continued to grow over the years reaching a 50 per cent deficit in 2008. This means that it takes 1.5 years

for the Earth to regenerate the renewable resources that people use, and absorb the CO2 waste they produce, in that same year. Just as it is possible to withdraw money from a bank account faster than to wait for the interest this money generates, renewable resources can be harvested faster than they can be re-grown. But just like overdrawing from a bank account, eventually the resource will be depleted.

Notice that overpopulation is never mentioned. The apparent assumption is that we can stop this on an individual level or with greater conservation efforts. World Wildlife Fund is absolutely correct in their bleak assessment of how our resource "accounts" are being overdrawn, but fails to explain its undeniable connection to human numbers. The website continues:

> At present, people are often able to shift their sourcing when this happens; however at current consumption rates, these sources will eventually run out of resources too—and some ecosystems will collapse even before the resource is completely gone.

Unfortunately, it is left to the reader to figure out that current consumption rates are driven by the billions of us now inhabiting Planet Earth. Our global growth rate further exacerbates the situation and it is not mentioned either. WWF does not take the opportunity to educate its members about overpopulation or growth. If they would take it to the next step and tell the blunt truth that we are overpopulated and using up our resources, many more would start to understand why so many species are endangered.

Greenpeace is known for its bold acts to save whales and rainforests. Apparently it is easier to challenge ships on the high seas than it is to include an overpopulation message on their website. Instead, their website states that: "All around the world, our oceans are in crisis. Three quarters of global fish stocks are suffering from overfishing and 90% of top marine predators are already gone." Here is another example of failing to connect the dots for people about what drives the overfishing. By not citing overpopulation as the culprit, Greenpeace offers inadequate solutions while the global population probably increases by another 220 million people per day!

They plan to use your donations for the next three years to:

1. Continue to change seafood choices made at . . . the wholesale level by working with supermarket retailers to make sustainable seafood the only choice available.

2. Convince governments and the United Nations that marine reserves are critical to the oceans' future—especially advocating setting aside 40% of the world's oceans as marine reserves.
3. Ensure that the Obama administration uses its diplomatic leverage to close the loopholes and end all commercial whaling.

This list contains no effort to help stop population growth and reduce human numbers. Donors are not educated about the driving force behind overfishing. Greenpeace USA and Greenpeace International are failing their own mission. Perhaps they don't get this issue or are afraid their donations will decline if they do. Regardless, they are making things worse. Visitors to their website are going to feel good about doing something even though it doesn't address the root cause of these problems. Their donors receive a false message about solutions that will never work without a concerted attempt to humanely reduce Homo sapiens' numbers. They leave the overpopulation issue to population groups to solve.

When we didn't fully understand the seriousness of the smoking issue, we came up with inadequate ways of addressing it. Once, there were smoking sections in the backs of airplanes. This is a great example of a response that didn't fully comprehend the total issue. The dangers of secondhand smoke had to be thoroughly researched and explained for years before people bought the concept. The secondhand effects of overpopulation are also challenging to comprehend, but not impossible, especially if conservation groups strongly assert this critical message.

The Monterey Bay Aquarium has a huge commitment to conservation, particularly of ocean fish. It developed an elaborate, informative guide about which fish to eat and which to avoid. But if you examine their website, you will be hard-pressed to see any reference to overpopulation causing overconsumption of fish. Imagine what would happen on our planet of over 7 billion if a newly discovered, tasty fish became popular. Advertise it on billboards and the fish's fate is sealed.

When McDonald's launched Fish Bites, their new 'McFood' product, it received an Eco-label from the Marine Stewardship Council. That is because McDonald's is to be complimented for going out of its way to select Alaska pollock as the source of this unhealthy fast food menu item. This wild-caught fish is currently on the Council's list of species with populations healthy enough to sustain fishing. Few are asking how long any species can be sustainably fished in an overpopulated and growing world. What if the marketing plan for this McMenu item succeeds like their hamburgers? Goodbye Alaska pollock.

In October of 2012, there was a conference called "Imagine International Conference on Cooperative Economics" at the International Summit of Cooperatives in Quebec City, Canada. These co-op enthusiasts came up with five postulates, the last reading, "The economy is a subsystem of a larger and finite system, the biosphere, hence permanent growth is impossible." How very true, but that is where it ends. This was another lost opportunity to educate people about human numbers. Our co-ops are already full of families with more than the sustainable number of children who do not understand how shopping at a co-op cannot make up for overpopulation

Aid for Africa, a charity alliance of US-based nonprofits, recently announced that lion populations are rapidly decreasing, so they are trying to save land for lions. This is another well-intended goal, but it will ultimately fail on a continent with the fastest growing population in the world. The pressure of growing populations on wildlife will always trump the ability to preserve land in the long term.

People need open land and their growing numbers turn forests into cropland faster than conservationists can fence their boundaries. Environmental legislation to set aside land is not worth the paper it is written on in an overpopulated country. Growing populations encroach on the land and it eventually succumbs to development. Ask the activists in Belize who tried to save a rainforest where scarlet macaws nested from a dam construction project. The demand for electricity was too great and the rainforest was destroyed.

This reality is largely ignored because saving the environment is compartmentalized between those who know how to navigate the territory of land saving and those who work on saving individual species. It is further divided between those who work in the political realm of mineral rights and those who set hunting regulations. These well-meaning groups work on their own, isolated from one another. Few are connected to each other, let alone to the issue which would permit their long-term success: the overpopulation issue.

The Wilderness Act of 1964 was established to protect wildlife, but setting aside enough untrammeled land is a challenge because land becomes more expensive when populations are hemorrhaging. That alone will not protect wildlife because overpopulation will encroach on the land in some fashion. When populations swell on nearby lands, laws get weakened and violators are no longer prosecuted. Pollution and invasive species become a problem too.

If you are a nature lover, then Jane Goodall is one of your heroes, pure and simple. She does so much to champion the needs of chimpanzees. Their numbers in western Africa have dwindled from about three million to 300,000 since she began her good work. Here is an excerpt from the Jane Goodall Institute about their mission and goals:

- Improve global understanding and treatment of great apes through research, public education and advocacy.
- Contribute to the preservation of great apes and their habitats by combining conservation with education and promotion of sustainable livelihoods in local communities.
- Create a worldwide network of young people who have learned to care deeply for their human community, for all animals and for the environment, and who will take responsible action to care for them.

I know that Dr. Goodall fully understands the overpopulation issue from her writings, her interviews and meetings with overpopulation activists. The absence of any overpopulation facts on the Institute's website is a testament to the controversy the issue brings with it. She knows that rising populations around the Gombe National Park will forever provide the impetus to kill these amazing animals for bush meat and short-circuit the future of her beloved chimps.

Overpopulation is so misunderstood that being upfront about it often assures that donations will dry up. It is much more lucrative to focus fundraising on downstream issues like education, research and the creation of caring communities than on trying to curb human populations, the true answer for long-term success.

Every conservation group from the Wilderness Society to Conservation International, from the Nature Conservancy to the National Wildlife Federation and many more, work on the issues they know well, the territory familiar to them. They may get it within their boardroom walls, but seem afraid of losing big donors by messaging about overpopulation in their fundraising efforts.

Sometimes avoiding the overpopulation issue is more deliberate. In 2004, math wizard David Gelbaum, who made his fortune on Wall Street, contributed $101 million to the Sierra Club. Under Carl Pope's direction, the Sierra Club took the bribe and followed Gelbaum's wishes that they not touch the immigration issue as it related to US population growth.

Early in 2013, the US State Department, under Hillary Rodham Clinton, censored an essay by Bindi Irwin, daughter of the late

Australian conservationist Steve Irwin. It seems she wrote about something so dreadful that the State Department refused to allow her submission as written. She wrote about overpopulation. She said it was all a lot like having a birthday party for 15 people and 70 people show up. You have 15 party favors, 15 cupcakes and when 70 people arrive they expect their fair share, but there isn't enough to go around. It was a great metaphor and very creative on this young activist's part. She should be commended for refusing to rewrite her essay and omit any reference to overpopulation.

This deliberate censorship demonstrates that our government is also afraid of raising awareness about the overpopulation issue.

Conservation groups typically do not know the jargon, politics or intricacies of the overpopulation issue. They do not work with human numbers, the median numbers of children per family or the math regarding overshoot of resources, even if these numbers are closely tied to their issue.

We live in a fragmented paradigm where each conservation arena is addressed by different NGOs. Understandably, they stay downstream in places they know well but their help to increase worldwide understanding is desperately needed.

What is not understandable is lying by omission to people by leaving out overpopulation entirely. The Nature Conservancy has an "Urgent Issues" column on its website. These urgent issues include protecting migratory birds, coral reefs and even climate change but overpopulation is not included. That is their first lie by omission. Click on "Climate Change" under the "Urgent Issues" column and you will find the following quote "People + Nature = Solutions", claiming that by protecting nature we can improve people's lives and provide solutions for a changing planet. There is no way you can have long-term solutions by protecting nature alone. You cannot improve people's lives unless you first admit that we have exceeded our planet's limits in human-carrying capacity.

The Nature Conservancy is part of a huge smoke and mirrors game played by way too many NGOs. Their messaging prevents nature-loving people from realizing that we have an overpopulation problem. I asked a family friend who donates to groups like this if he knew how many people are added to the planet each year. As a donor and member of several, he said he had no idea. I told him that it wasn't entirely his fault, but rather the fault of environmental organizations that omit overpopulation facts as a part of their overall message.

Rainforest protection organizations are made up of very passionate people who love the rainforest and its biodiversity like I do.

They will be hard-pressed to save anything but forest remnants when the countries with the remaining rainforest regions have populations which will double in 20 years. When four million people become eight million people, conservation laws will fall by the wayside.

Bolivia, one of South America's poorest countries, is a perfect example. It is rich in rainforests but threatened by a fertility rate of 4.8 children per woman which translates to a 27 year doubling rate. So in 27 years instead of about 10 million people trying to eke out a living within their boundaries, Bolivia will be wrestling with 20 million even more impoverished people with less forest, less fresh water and other needed resources to share.

How sad that a website search of groups from the Rainforest Action Network to the Rainforest Alliance uncovers no references to overpopulation. In fact, they also tell a lie by giving you only limited options which they say will save the rainforest. Choose certified products, join their organization and make a donation are some of their suggestions. This just isn't true. It is another noble effort falling short of what really needs to be done. Yes, they certify rainforest products, but this will do 'bupkas' (Yiddish for nothing), without checking population growth and helping to humanely reduce human numbers.

The Center for Biodiversity is rare in its bold attempts to raise awareness on the taboo subject of overpopulation. They have many campaigns to raise awareness about overpopulation. The Center has a creative Crowded Planet campaign which solicits photos from people to share what living on a planet of 7.2 billion feels like.

Nature photographers are also very passionate about their subject matter. Most consider themselves conservationists. The very talented Jim Brandenburg has a separate foundation to support prairie restoration.

These dedicated individuals work very hard making a living capturing the beauty of natural landscapes, bears, wolves, bobcats and animals most will never see in the wild. Their gorgeous books and calendars make the world a more beautiful place, but many take a pass at educating the world about the precarious situation these amazing animals face because of human overpopulation.

With the exception of Craig Blacklock from Moose Lake Minnesota, I would argue that most nature photographers are just creating more mourners. There will now be more people grieving when the last polar bear takes its breath. The message is that loving wildlife and buying coffee table nature books and a T-shirt from a supportive organization will help preserve animals, and it just isn't true. The message that more people just equals less wildlife is not touched.

Modern humans take up too much room to allow adequate wilderness to support numerous species, especially the big animals. Species that start to recover must face human resistance. Coyotes and gray wolves get into trouble because they adapt to human encroachment by eating pets and frightening unappreciative citizens with their presence.

I no longer attend an event which used to give me great solace. The Living Green Expo was held annually in St. Paul, Minnesota. I have encouraged its various leaders to help educate people about overpopulation. Instead, they give out delusional messages, misleading people into thinking that simply buying bamboo flooring, supporting organic growers and someday providing affordable solar power will make everything well with the world. People leave smiling, their recycled-content cloth bags filled with organic soaps and sustainable snacks in tow, inspired to join other eco-minded warriors on a mission to be greener.

All the green light bulbs and organic produce in the world won't keep us from falling off the resource cliff. This feel-good event sends a false and ultimately dangerous message.

I thought of a remedy: Have a laptop computer at the entrance cued to the website where a world population clock records the current population on the planet. It adds 144 numbers each minute, which is quite remarkable. Each participant would be asked to predict what the world population number would be on the clock by the time they leave the Expo. They could win a free energy saving light bulb if they came within 100 of the correct number. This idea would be easy and inexpensive to implement. One person is needed to monitor the contest. Each visitor would be given a resource information sheet so they would leave the Expo realizing that unless and until we work to reduce births on the planet, U.S. and elsewhere, we cannot call ourselves truly green. Those who run the event, and there have been several agencies, have always had an excuse why this couldn't be done. The latest incarnation of this event is called Minnesota Goes Green. I offered to staff a booth there on behalf of World Population Balance in the spring of 2014. I said I would fit into their format as well as offering to pay. After several ignored emails and phone calls it was clear that they were not interested in having overpopulation groups anywhere near their event.

Comparing websites through the lens of overpopulation is illuminating. I am a member of The Izaak Walton League, a conservation organization that understands the connection of population and conservation. It is one of the few that is willing to post statements like the following:

> When it comes to affecting natural resources, most of us think about consumption first. Energy efficiency, water quality, and recycling receive much attention. However, the number of people—and how fast that number is growing—is just as important. More people require more services, consume more resources, and produce more waste—placing greater demands on land, water, schools, roads, and utilities.

While courageous compared to other groups, IWL chapters are inconsistent in supporting such statements. Many don't instill an appropriate sense of urgency to concentrate our efforts on the core issue of overpopulation. Recently, they have moved overpopulation to the back burner while focusing their efforts on the downstream issues of fracking and sulfide mining. Fracking and sulfide mining are awful but stopping these attempts to squeeze out the last drop of fuel will be only temporary until overpopulation is seriously addressed.

The distinguished nature photographer Craig Blacklock is outspoken on the overpopulation issue, advocating for families to commit to having just one child as he has. He routinely writes about this issue and brings it up when he is hired to give presentations. Craig's concern about overpopulation is palpable. Every time he discusses the increased traffic and timber harvesting in northern Minnesota, he attaches it directly to Minnesota's growing population. He says that the best gift he can give his only daughter is to NOT give her a sibling. I hope more will take his lead.

The Rewilding Institute is to be commended for its position on overpopulation. With Dave Foreman at the helm, they focus on urgent issues, including human population growth. The Institute's website states, "The massive growth in the human population through the 20th century has had more impact on biodiversity than any other single factor".

Foreman's book, *Man Swarm and the Killing of Wildlife* is powerful. In it, Foreman puts the demise of wildlife right in the lap of overpopulation. He unabashedly accuses people of ignoring the "unbearable load a mounting human population places atop wild nature."

Many conservation organizations have refused to carry Foreman's forward-thinking book as a recommended title, again proving their unwillingness to address human overpopulation. Unfortunately, groups like The Nature Conservancy, with net assets of over five billion dollars, are a much bigger voice than groups with much smaller budgets.

The Center for Biological Diversity also connects the dots on overpopulation. Their website devotes an entire page to educating people about the population issue. They state, "Unsustainable human population growth is an essential root cause to the crisis."

This brave NGO launched the Endangered Species Condom Project to make the connection between human numbers and species protection. They created quite a stir with "Wrap with care, save the polar bear" condoms along with others. My favorite is "In the sack? Save the leatherback." Their creativity and humor is commendable. There are hundreds of conservation organizations in the U.S. and many with international offices. Imagine the way they could help educate wildlife lovers if they were to be honest with their members about what is causing so much distress in the world of wildlife protection.

Chapter 5

Reaching Out to Social Justice Activists

Smart Growth destroys the environment, dumb
growth destroys the environment. The only
difference is that Smart Growth does it with good
taste. It's like booking passage on the Titanic.
Whether you go first class or steerage the result is
the same.

—Al Bartlett

The human rights movement has not embraced overpopulation because it appears antithetical to their beliefs. Some of these social justice activists have even vehemently opposed overpopulation as a concept and dismissed its activists as being racists. Madeline Weld, President of Population Institute of Canada, points out that the Southern Poverty Law Center and the Center for New Community are aggressive in maligning those concerned with overpopulation. These human rights organizations deny the claim that there are too many people on the planet. They fear it will be used as leverage against people who are disadvantaged. They need to see that the opposite is true. Overpopulation sets the stage for injustice because it creates a scarcity of resources that leads to inequality.

Water.org, actor Matt Damon's organization, believes, "everyone in the world should have sustainable and affordable access to safe water and sanitation. To get there, we must fundamentally change the system. And this change must be driven by the intrinsic power of the poor as customers and citizens." It is interesting to note that their projects are all in the seriously overpopulated countries of India,

Haiti, Ethiopia, Bangladesh, Kenya and Uganda. I try imagining my home state of Minnesota with the population density of one of these countries. As of this writing we have 5.3 million people. We would have 79 million people if Minnesota's population density equaled that of Haiti. I would be calling Matt Damon to help us get water too, but only after calling on an overpopulation group to help stabilize and humanely decrease our numbers.

As a committed activist, actor Sean Penn spends a good deal of time in Haiti assisting recovery from devastating earthquakes. This Oscar-winning actor once said, "My job is to help people get the future they want to have." Haiti is overpopulated today and continues to grow. Several observers have referred to Haiti as a failed state. From 1950 to 2050, if no one interferes, Haiti will almost quadruple its population density per square mile, according to forecasts by the United Nations Population Funds, UNFPA. If these famous activists remain silent on addressing Haiti's serious overpopulation problem, the harm from increased human density will offset their good intentions.

The Clinton Foundation funds COTAP (Carbon Offsets to Alleviate Poverty) in Malawi in sub-Saharan South Africa with the mission of planting trees to employ impoverished people while offsetting corporate carbon emissions. It is notably creative to combine solutions to several problems in a single project. According to COTAP's website, they are concerned about the project's long-term goals and want the project to be locally sustainable. To do that they are actively training individuals on the values of the trees and the decentralization of the tree nurseries is their long-term strategy.

Nowhere on COTAP's website is the following data. This is a densely populated, land-locked country with only 36,367 square miles of land currently struggling to feed, clothe and educate well over 15.91 million inhabitants (2012). Malawi has a growth rate which has doubled its population since 2000, making it the most densely populated country in Africa. These facts would make it clear that with more and more people living unsustainably in this country, the viability of planting trees for this project is limited. Another issue is that most Malawians heat with wood and charcoal. The immediate need for sources of firewood will also put an ever-increasing pressure on this project. If no one at COTAP steps up to the overpopulation plate, Malawi will have 20 million people by 2025. They will struggle to exist in a landscape where the Clinton Foundation employed farmers to plant trees but neglected to also work on helping Malawians to humanely reach a sustainable population.

Overpopulation is not just in the blind spot of NGOs like COTAP. Many world leaders have a very hard time seeing overpopulation as the root cause of their problems. The Malawian Minister of Economic Planning and Development Ralph Jooma said in November 2013 that he is concerned that many Malawians are trapped in abject poverty. Jooma also stated that his government's vision is that by 2020, Malawi, "as a God-fearing nation, will be secure, democratically mature, environmentally sustainable, self-reliant with equal opportunities for and active participation by all." Such noble goals are impossible to achieve without addressing the cold hard facts that too many Malawians are struggling to survive in a country lacking adequate resources for them.

People do not lack compassion over human suffering. They do lack a deep understanding of the source of these problems. Efforts to help alleviate environmental problems are often in the form of laws which try their best to protect vital habitat. Malawi has enacted many: the Environmental Management Act of 1996, the Forestry Policy of 1996, the Land Policy of 2002, the Water and Sanitation Policy of 2005, and the Biodiversity Strategy and Action Plan of 2008. None of them will work in the long term because they cannot offset the way its growing population undermines attempts to save the environment.

Bill Clinton wrote the foreword to *Hearts on Fire, Stories of Visionaries Igniting Idealism into Action*, a book by Jill W. Iscol and Peter W. Cookson, Jr. It details the lives of heroic individuals who overcame great obstacles to reach out and help others. The authors intended the book to be inspirational but it made me shake my head in disappointment. In his forward, Clinton said, "[It] has been my mission to help create a world of shared benefits and shared responsibilities, where poverty is reduced, hunger is eliminated, and opportunity for making a better life is available to everyone." He expressed the heart of the human rights movement. The problem is that these noble ideals are futile in the context of overpopulation.

The Jolie-Pitt Foundation founded by actors Angelina Jolie and Brad Pitt, states that the organization envisions, "The end of human suffering in The Horn of Africa through the creation of an environment where people are self-reliant, living in a sustainable and prosperous community with the assurance of a victimless future." That is a lovely statement, but nowhere is it clear that these activists understand what a sustainable community means. The online magazine *Think Africa Press*, in article 14, Sept. 2011 states the reality: "The sustained and rapid population growth occurring in the Horn of Africa raises serious concerns over food supply." According to John Omiti, principal policy analyst at the Kenya Institute for Public

Policy Research and Analysis, "Population growth is higher than our ability to produce food. We need to address the demographic challenge to balance supply and demand."

This is not mentioned anywhere on the Jolie-Pitt Foundation website, articles or links. These activists will ultimately fail by ignoring overpopulation as a core reason for the suffering of those they attempt to serve.

The United States constantly interferes in the business of other countries, whether trying to acquire their resources, securing votes at the United Nations or establishing political alliances. We have military bases in 63 countries, yet somehow it crosses a moral line to get involved with the population growth rates of foreign countries. The U.S. gave 225 million dollars in foreign aid to Haiti in 2007 when its population was 8.71 million. None of those dollars were tied to a commitment to reduce births in Haiti. By 2013, Haiti's population grew to over 10 million people. Meanwhile, activists from the nongovernmental world send pencils, school books, and mattresses. They avoid the one thing that could reduce Haiti's poverty. What Haiti really needs is a comprehensive culturally appropriate family planning and education program to reduce family sizes.

Groups focused on ending hunger are some of the worst violators of what I call "population sanity". Behaving with population sanity requires understanding that you cannot "Feed My Starving Children" without curbing population. You simply end up with more starving children. These well-intentioned groups contribute to the future food insecurity in countries where they do not also work to humanely lower birth rates.

The Feed My Starving Children website claims that nutrition will solve the world's problems, because that alone will permit health, education and jobs. This is not true because without measures to reduce the birth rate, nutrition will lead to more population growth in places unable to support any more people. There are approximately 200,000 people seeking food security today who did not exist yesterday. Feed My Starving Children ignores the ultimate results of feeding people in an environment that cannot sustain them long-term. They do not measure the number of people a landscape can support, and they help perpetuate unsustainable numbers until the next disaster strikes. If groups like Feed My Starving Children want to really improve the condition of the poor, they would partner with population groups and design companion birth control and family planning programs.

The United Nations Millennium Project undertook a bold initiative to end poverty by 2015. This is desirable, but there is no way to eliminate poverty through donations, redistribution of wealth or the most innovative program the UN proposes. The only way to make progress toward the elimination of poverty is to do what restaurant owner and activist Mechai Viravaidya did in his homeland of Thailand. Beginning in the 1970s, he worked on population stabilization and reduction. Mechai saw so much poverty in his beloved country but he did not focus his efforts directly on solving poverty. Instead he tried to reduce the average birth rate per woman by helping his countrymen, women and children get comfortable with the one device that would get them out of poverty: the condom. He made his waiters at his restaurant wear them on their heads, turned them into centerpieces on his tables and even started a "cops and rubbers" program. He was successful in getting cab drivers to hand them out as well as officers. He was tireless in his promotion of the value of condoms and small family planning and he was successful. Women went from averaging over 7 children to just under two. Nine million pregnancies were prevented and the poverty that would have gone hand in hand with all of those hungry mouths to feed.

The Bill and Melinda Gates Foundation has a strong family planning directive. The Foundation's website states that family planning is directly related to issues of poverty and women's health. I was confused that they didn't take it a step further and say that overpopulation is the real problem we are facing on this planet. Watching an interview with Bill Gates revealed that the Foundation focuses on empowering individual women because he believes that poverty causes overpopulation, therefore solving poverty will by default cure overpopulation in its wake. There is an undeniable correlation between rich and poor countries when it comes to how many children people have. Richer countries tend to have lower birthrates and poorer countries tend to have higher birthrates. Yes, it is less of a political landmine to work on poverty, but the evidence is pretty clear. It is just far simpler, easier, cheaper and more realistic to focus on reducing the number of births than to try to help families make a better living. The U.S. spends millions on foreign aid and has little to show for our ability to help fast growing developing countries to get out of poverty. Canada also spends a lot on foreign aid with poor results. In 2007 they issued a report that after 45 years of total development aid to sub-Saharan Africa totaling 575 billion in US dollars, many people are worse off than they once were. (Canada Senate Committee report Feb. 2007) While some of that failure may be due to corruption, it still demonstrates that the practice of trying to lift people out of poverty with the donation of money is a failing proposition. Examining the effectiveness of foreign aid as it is would be a great political platform for an insightful candidate especially if they suggest a completely different approach of working to keep population in check with resources.

Mechai Viravaidya, who is often referred to as the "condom king" in his native Thailand, would also disagree with the "poverty causes overpopulation" approach. He has a great track record of doing just the opposite. Viravaidya said: "Now, when I was a young man, 40 years ago, the country was very, very poor with lots and lots and lots of people living in poverty. We decided to do something about it, but we didn't begin with a welfare program or a poverty reduction program. We began with a family planning program and it worked on both accounts."

Chapter 6

An Invitation to Feminists

It's not just the religious right that hampers
access to family planning . . . so does the
feminist and social justice left . . . They derailed
any direct targeting of population growth by
linking it to indifference to women's rights, racism
and eugenics.

Madeline Weld

Bill Reyerson, president of Population Media Center, has devoted his life to finding clever and socially responsible ways to reduce population in developing countries. He knows firsthand how reduced family size can help alleviate poverty and conserve resources. His organization creates soap operas to influence family size choices using entertainment as a strategy to shift people's behavior. He has learned over the years that even if you could offer free and accessible family planning clinics in every village and on every street corner, even if you could empower all of the women, the average family size will not be reduced. The key thing that must change in order for birth control and women's empowerment to work to is to change the cultural expectation of family size. Reyerson illustrates this point by stating that, "Many, if not most, societies demand that a woman must bear her husband a son. Moreover, many societies have a cultural expectation that a married couple will produce a large number of children. In Madagascar, the ideal family size is 14 children (seven sons and seven daughters); on average in sub-Saharan Africa, ideal family size is five children." These expectations have no tie to ecological realities and little to do with access to birth control.

Culture is a tricky thing. It cannot be legislated. Reyerson and his talented staff have learned that to change cultural expectations the societal narrative must be altered. In Mexico his mentor Miguel Sabido created a soap opera called *Acompaname*, or *Come with Me*. The show focused on the importance of family planning. According to Ryerson, there was a 23% increase in contraceptive sales in one year. Over the next decade the stories on the family planning soap operas helped Mexico's birth rate to decline by 34%.

Radio is another medium which can be effective in changing the cultural expectations of family size. Working in African communities with no television access, radio broadcasts are used. As in most situations, solutions are multi-pronged. There are rarely silver bullets, particularly on the overpopulation issue. Change the culture without affordable birth control and women's empowerment and it will not work. Empower women and provide birth control without changing the societal pressure each woman has on her reproductive choices and that will fail as well. This is where we are today. A culturally dominant false belief in the impact empowerment of women and access to birth control alone will have on overpopulation. The incredible challenge before activists is to get people to let go of deeply engrained belief systems and accept that modern day realities dictate the need for drastic changes in cultural reproductive practice.

I invite feminists to broaden their focus. I invite them to see that they are two-thirds on target but are missing a critical piece. The remaining third is key to their own success. Their heroic efforts must incorporate an overpopulation narrative. The marriage of women's empowerment, access to birth control and culturally changing expected family size due to our global overpopulation problem would be a much more effective road to follow. True empowerment of women can only happen on a sustainable planet. Historically, abuse of second-class citizens increases when resources become scarce. In the chaos that follows overpopulation-induced resource scarcity, women and children will be the first to suffer.

Feminists work on critically important issues. That is why I have considered myself a feminist since high school when I had a poster in my room that said, "A woman without a man is like a fish without a bicycle". It was a perfect poster for a future naturalist. Unfortunately, women still struggle against male oppression as evidenced by everything from the rise in sexual assault on campuses and in the military, to gender inequality in sports and the job market. Objectification of women in the media is still a problem and now feminists are called upon to fight sex trade and sex abuse. A woman is abused every six seconds in the U.S., an issue that should turn all of us into feminists.

Feminists must continue their fight to protect women in a world that continues to brutalize them. Population activists, however, are the friends of feminists, not the enemies. Their efforts are not an attempt to control their freedom, only a desire to improve their lives and the future of the children they do bring into this world. Feminists need to listen to scientists and overpopulation experts, who are warning of food and water shortages, biodiversity loss and increasing conflict. They are telling us that we need to stabilize and reduce human numbers now if we are ever to achieve sustainability. Women will be the first to benefit in a world with a sustainable population.

It is very important to give women choice and access to birth control, but in the context of overpopulation it will never be enough. Some newly empowered women may indeed choose to have fewer children, but choosing four instead of ten will still be unsustainable. Women and men must be supported and informed about the impact the size of their family has on the planet's ability to support future generations. In addition to women's empowerment we must change our narrative about the critical need for living sustainably on our planet.

Most women in our country have a choice to pick their family size. They often pick an unsustainable number for reasons having little to do with empowerment or access to safe birth control methods. Choice of family size in America is based on a combination of issues including economics, age, medical issues, personal preference, religious background and family traditions. The U.S. needs its own multimedia campaign to demonstrate the benefits of family size reduction. Empowering women is important and desirable, but it alone will not solve this mega-issue. We are rendering our planet lifeless by our unsustainable numbers and habits. This reality should be our society's primary focus.

Only with encouragement from education policies and narrative-altering media about the critical need for humane population reduction will women be truly empowered. Rights of the subjugated cannot survive on an overpopulated planet. The earth must be able to sustain us too. If we worry about only our rights then we will not be around long enough to enjoy the justice we worked so hard to attain. If we achieve sustainability but still subjugate women, then we will have lost too. We must join forces and recognize the value that each has in improving the world.

I realize that it will require a shift in consciousness for many feminists to come to terms with my argument. Their worldview will need to be broadened to include the impact of growth as well as the freedom of choice for individual women. Overpopulation hurts women, impairs prosperity and condemns them to poverty in many countries and robs their children of a promising future. Matching resources with a sustainable demand is deeply humane. Otherwise mothers will continue to needlessly suffer as they watch their children struggle. This issue needs to be rethought and discussed thoroughly until the truth emerges. Only then will feminists be able to see that caring about people means working to eliminate overpopulation, wherever it exists, as humanely as we can and as rapidly as we are able.

Let me demonstrate how these are mistakenly tied together and why empowerment of women is not the silver bullet to ending our overpopulation crisis. If the Bill & Melinda Gates Foundation is successful and brings birth control information and access to all women who currently need it, an estimated 75 million annual births would be avoided. That would be wonderful on so many levels and will take care of our current growth problem. Unfortunately, it will not rid us of our overpopulation problem because, as mentioned in chapter two, population momentum will still send world population to over 9 billion, a number that exceeds our resource base by over 6 billion people. Without alerting newly empowered women about how our world is so desperately overpopulated, numbers will not reverse in time to avert disaster.

In other words, if we allow human numbers to increase toward 8 and 10 billion, women will become even more defined by their poverty, forced to carry water and wood from longer distances. Women, already second-class citizens in so many countries, will be even more abused as resources run dry. Empowerment will be a long-lost dream.

In 2012, Madeline Weld, president of Population Institute Canada, stated in her article, *Deconstructing the dangerous dogma of denial: the feminist-environmental justice movement and its flight from overpopulation*, that:

> At the Cairo conference in 1994, the world fled from numbers. But, as current events in Cairo and elsewhere are showing, we cannot flee from the consequences of those numbers. The Marxist feminist/social justice ideology that denies the population factor and vilifies those who address it is as long-lived as some of the dictators in the Arab world and, like them, finds itself on shaky ground, because ideology cannot trump reality. An ideology that claims to promote social justice, but does not recognize that the Earth is finite, is more than unethical.

Weld goes on to ask,

> Does ethics operate in a vacuum or are we obligated to con-
> sider the consequences of our ethical choices? Does the right
> of a woman to have as many children as she chooses trump the
> right of her own and other people's descendants to have a livable
> environment? Does it trump the right of the global community
> in general to live on a healthy planet? Do those of us now living
> have any obligations to husband resources for future genera-
> tions? Does the human species have any ethical obligations to
> non-human life—to protect Earth's biodiversity?

Feminist issues are often conflated with overpopulation issues, but
they are not the same. The clear message of the overpopulation camp
is that we are overwhelming our resources with our numbers to the
detriment of current and future generations. Nowhere in that message
is there a mention of abortion or women's rights. The issue has been
co-opted by those with other agendas. Feminists attending the 1994
Cairo International Conference on Population and Development
(ICPD) saw an opportunity to forward their agenda of women's
empowerment. The ICPD was convened under the auspices of the
United Nations. More than 180 countries took part in finalizing a
Programme of Action in the area of population and development for
the next 20 years. The feminists were successful in shifting the outcomes of the conference. Instead of an action plan to sound the alarm
of the disasters created by population growth, the conference moved
downstream and called attention to the need for the empowerment of
women.

This shift in priorities created ill feelings among population
groups who knew the overall problem of overpopulation was not going to be fully addressed by a switch to women's issues. They also knew
that though there would be many conferences convened to address
women's issues, there would never be another chance to catch the rise
of population. In 1994 the global population was 5.6 billion, almost
2 billion less than it is today. Feminists refocused the conference to be
about women's empowerment under what Madeline Weld labeled as
their "Marxist feminist/social justice ideology." As a result, the population movement lost much of its steam and has never fully recovered.

Protecting biodiversity is not only about ethics. It is about our
very survival. It is the big picture. Feminists working downstream do
not connect to this issue. The richer the biodiversity the more resilient
humans are on the planet. Just one of many examples is the need for

diverse populations of bees. They will be more resistant to disease and they are critical for pollination of many food crops.

We are all familiar with empowered women with large families. Dare I mention Representative Michele Bachmann and former Alaska Governor Sarah Palin? No one can deny that these two women are greatly empowered and that no one denies them access to birth control, yet between them, they have contributed eleven children to our overpopulated planet. Large families are not exclusive to Republicans, of course. Nancy Pelosi, former Democratic Speaker of the House of Representatives, has five children. Choosing large families transcends politics. I know many women who are very liberal. They shop at co-ops, live low on the food chain and off the power grid, yet have two children or more. They have not heard the message about the ecological need to reduce births below replacement. No one is telling them in a loud and clear voice that the Earth, both developed and underdeveloped, is overpopulated relative to its resource base. They are not aware that the problems their children will face growing up will be based on this grim reality.

Truly empowered women will be inspired to fight for population stabilization as a women's issue.

The good news is that when totally informed about issues, people can make the right choices. When chemists Sherwood Rowland and Mario Molina discovered that aerosol sprays released chloroflurocarbons (CFCs) which could rise to the stratosphere and destroy the earth's protective ozone layer, Americans responded. The sales of these products plummeted before all of the CFC bans were in place.

I believe people will become creative and find ways to nurture children without having to have their own large families. One idea is to promote the idea of guide-parents, a form of god-parenthood. These are adults who help to nurture and raise one child together and who in turn will be supported in old age.

It is critical that we find the courage to tell the truth about the future children will face if the planet remains overpopulated. True empowerment starts from knowing the whole truth. With forecasts of economic and environmental collapse in the near future, how many people would want to bring children into the world?

In the last few decades, "family planning" has become the politically more acceptable term to birth control. Family planning organizations focus their attention on providing birth control to women in need, but have glossed over the overpopulation issue. Overpopulation has become too politically charged and they want to concentrate their funding efforts on helping women who would otherwise bring unwanted children into the world. Overpopulation is a global issue while family planning organizations work at the individual level. They do amazing work helping individual women to make healthy choices about family size and how far apart their children are spaced. Finding a way to help them spread the realities about overpopulation, while still helping individuals, is the challenge.

Access to birth control is, undoubtedly, a key pathway towards birth reduction. Right now, just having access to birth control is not enough to stop the train wreck of a growing population of 7.2 billion. Stopping at two is not enough. The overwhelming truth is that overpopulation is eating up our resources and setting the stage for catastrophe. People must be educated that unless we humanely encourage the choice of one-child families with access to birth control, we will not be able to reduce the misery and suffering headed our way as our already unsustainable populations continue to rise.

Chapter 7

Religion on Trial
WWJD?

Too many people have died in the name of
Christ for anyone to heed the call.

—Graham Nash

Our religious stories give us permission to do what we are doing to the planet. If your core belief is that the Earth is a temporary holding tank before your true destination of heaven, then taking care of the Earth is not important. If you believe that the apocalypse is real but divinely predicted, you will not get involved. Religions also cloud our ability to think critically about the science behind all of the warnings scientists are giving us about what is happening to our climate and resources.

When it comes to overpopulation, what would Jesus, Moses, Mohammed, or other religious figures do? What instruction is there in the Old Testament, the New Testament or the Koran about how to deal with the problems caused by overpopulation? This is of course a trick question. There are no references in religious texts about the issue of what to do when people overwhelm the limited resources of the planet for a very good reason. Most of today's organized religions go back thousands of years when the earth's population was in the millions. In fact 2,000 years ago there were 300 million people in the whole world. That is less than the current population of the U.S., which reached 320 million in 2015. Obviously this issue was of no concern and was not even imagined back when a few viruses or other natural disasters could have wiped out our entire species. Because of this, the clergy of today's churches and synagogues are not focused on overpopulation. Their sacred texts provide no guidance on this issue and neither do they.

I am intentionally using a very broad brush stroke when I lump all religions together. I realize there are cavernous differences between the various denominations. Progressive churches have green committees, welcome gay members and clergy and overall are the polar opposite of their conservative counterparts. Conservative churches often live in the dark ages of repression and want to discriminate against gays and people of color in the name of religion. Some are arcane about birth control and work to get Roe vs. Wade overturned because of their fervent hatred of abortion. Those that find birth control to be against God's will have long been the nemesis of population control advocates.

The reason I can lump these opposing groups together on some level is that no group is taking the lead or even paying much attention to overpopulation. A few progressive churches and synagogues have invited me to come and talk to select committees within their organizations, but that is the only difference between progressive and conservative denominations when it comes to taking on overpopulation as an issue they believe their parishioners should know and care about. When I met with one rabbi of a progressive Reform synagogue for an hour trying to convince her of my interest, as a Jew, to raise the awareness of this issue with her congregation, I was not even allowed to speak to their sustainability committee let alone take my turn at the pulpit.

In general, modern day organized religions are set up to teach us how to behave toward one another and how to honor their version of a supreme being. They provide a service by offering rituals which give meaning to life's transitions. We should not, however, give them the moral authority to dictate how to treat the planet when it comes to overpopulation because that is not their area of expertise. Indigenous people are the only ones who can look to their elders for guidance on how to relate to the earth because this issue is a part of their dominant narrative. We need to be looking at science and math for guidance on how we need to live on this limited planet of ours. Science can measure resources and predict when they will run out according to the demand placed on them. Love and compassion may indeed be limitless but copper, phosphorus, titanium, and a long list of others are not. We can pray as hard as we want, but the fact is that we are running out of the essential resources which help us to live in the modern world.

The world's major organized religions all have the same general anthropocentric heaven versus hell based narrative. Their rules are set up to help us negotiate how to relate to each other and to offer praise to the supreme being in charge of all life. In general, these powerful doctrines teach that humans are ironically the epitome of creation and yet not empowered to do much to change course.

Where religion does the most harm to the overpopulation issue is of course their pro-natalist views involving contraception and family size. The more fundamentalist the religion, the more fearful they seem to be about the very thought of stopping or even preventing a pregnancy at any stage or for any reason. The more conservative the religion the more they view every zygote as a god-inspired being which must be brought to life. A glaring example of this is the Duggar family of reality television's *19 Kids and Counting*. They believe that constant childbearing is a Christian obligation. There is even a new movement afoot in the evangelical Christian movement to eschew all contraception because of its potential to be an abortive device.

The other fundamentalist views which are extremely detrimental to the overpopulation issue are the belief that "His" plan is already in place and that we do not have the power to change it. The beliefs that disturb me the most are the ones that are apocalyptic and agree that the Earth's ability to support us will end someday soon due to a plan foretold in the Bible. They must hear the forecasts of resource collapse and smile with the satisfaction that the Bible was right.

The only narratives with an Earth-focused overarching story are that of the ancestor-focused, mother earth traditions of most indigenous peoples. If religion today would have embraced the teachings of the First Nation peoples, and put humans as a part of the web of life instead of on top of it, perhaps we wouldn't have gotten ourselves into this mess in the first place. Imagine being taught that humans are a part of the web of life and that what we do to the web we do to ourselves!

On its best day, religion inspires its followers to help the less fortunate and make the world a better place. Former president Jimmy Carter is a very religious man whose faith inspires him to work for organizations like Habitat for Humanity. If they were inspired by the overpopulation issue, perhaps they could direct their humanitarian work to bring about balanced populations in the world.

Years ago I belonged to an organization called MIEC, or Minnesota Interfaith Ecology Coalition. Before Earth Day each year it was our task to find environmentally inspired scripture and edicts from each denomination and send them out to the appropriate clergy. Our request was that a religiously appropriate ecological message would be preached on the Sunday before Earth Day. I remember researching messages for Catholic, Jewish, Presbyterian and Unitarian churches.

I think we were on the right track. Many people will listen to their clergy long before they listen to the likes of me, no matter how long I have studied this issue. The problem was that none of our messaging had to do with human numbers. It was all downstream advice about recycling and planting trees.

Churches often exercise their power to influence politics. Some churches were quite progressive in the 1960s on the overpopulation issue. According to Stephen Mumford, author of *Overcoming Overpopulation: The Rise and Fall of American Political Will*,

> [T]he General Assembly of the Presbyterian Church in 1965 urged "the government of the United States to be ready to assist countries who request help in the development of programs of voluntary planned parenthood as a practical and humane means of controlling fertility and population growth." By 1971, the General Assembly recognized that, "The assumption that couples have the freedom to have as many children as they can support should be challenged. We can no longer justify bringing into existence as many children as we desire. Our corporate responsibility to each other prohibits this." In 1972, the Presbyterians called on governments "to take such actions as will stabilize population size. We who are motivated by the urgency of overpopulation . . . would preserve the species by responding in faith: Do not multiply—the earth is filled!"

The 1960s was a time of great progress on this issue. President Nixon appointed John D. Rockefeller III to chair a commission on population growth. The 24-member commission wanted to pass a Population Education Act and establish sex education programs in the schools. The backlash to these progressive ideas was led by Catholic bishops who issued counterproposals in their "Pastoral Plan for Pro-Life Activities". The Pastoral Plan was issued on November 20, 1975, largely in response to the Supreme Court decision on abortion, Roe v. Wade. They launched a comprehensive campaign in all branches of government to make sure the political will to address population growth was killed.

President Nixon was prepared to embrace the overpopulation issue during his presidency but the Catholic Church made sure he knew there would be an incredible price to pay for following that path. He abandoned his efforts because of that political pressure. Mumford reported that in 1973, John D. Rockfeller said, "The greatest difficulty has been the very active opposition by the Roman Catholic Church through its various agencies in the United States."

Clergy retain a moral obligation to work on this issue, but today's climate is very different and extremely polarized. We must help leaders of faith communities understand our planetary predicament. They must realize that their downstream missions are an inadequate response to this crisis. If we do nothing to reduce the impact of overpopulation, we are complicit in the disasters it will cause. The gap between our planet's limited and declining supply of natural resources and the increasing demand for them sets the stage for incredible misery and suffering in the world. We can only redistribute resources so much. Our demand must be humanely reduced to set a new stage for a better world. Without a doubt, overpopulation is the most ignored moral issue of our time.

According to the Bureau of Labor Statistics in 2012, 44,000 clergy serving various denominations are employed in the U.S. These spiritual leaders should help guide their congregations toward a better, more just world. Long-term social justice is only possible when we stop straining the earth's resources beyond their capacity to provide for us. Justice will only thrive in a future where people and resources are balanced.

On August 27th, 1963, many rabbis, priests and ministers joined hands with the late Dr. Martin Luther King, Jr. in the cry for justice at the March on Washington. This key event in paving the way for the Civil Rights Act of 1964 had its roots in the faith community as a cry for social justice. I wonder if these clergy would have joined Dr. King if he would have organized a similar march to protect our resources from overpopulation. It is often easier to mobilize clergy for social justice than it is to get people excited about this issue. But perhaps Dr. King could have mobilized them by repeating the statement he prepared for the Margaret Sanger award ceremony in 1966: "Unlike plagues of the dark ages or contemporary diseases we do not yet understand, the modern plague of overpopulation is solvable by means we have discovered and with resources we possess. What is lacking is not sufficient knowledge of the solution but universal consciousness of the gravity of the problem and education of the billions who are its victims."

Duane L. Cady, professor of philosophy at Hamline University in St. Paul, Minnesota said, "Religions have significant influence in shaping how peoples ought to live, the fundamental focus of ethics." Religions as caretakers of our values could have a huge role to play in exposing the overpopulation issue. Unfortunately, the scientific reality of our own species exceeding carrying capacity runs counter to most religious doctrines.

In his paper *The Historical Roots of Our Ecological Crisis*, Professor Lynn Townsend White, Jr. states, "Christianity made it possible to exploit nature in a mood of indifference to the feelings of natural objects . . . It's the most anthropocentric religion the world has seen . . . what we do about ecology depends on our ideas of the man-nature relationship."

The world's dominant non-indigenous religions rely on ancient sacred texts for guidance. They originated from 4,000 years ago to 1400 years ago when overpopulation was not an issue. Their doctrines often have edicts of procreation which made sense when the world was less populated. Approximately 50 million people lived on the whole planet in 1000 BCE. The first billion of us did not arrive until 1804. In contrast, our yearly global growth of approximately 73 million exceeds the world's entire population 1,000 years before Christianity began.

The "be fruitful and multiply" edict is grounded in a time when it made sense. They also come from a faraway place, the Middle East. To paraphrase David W. Orr's book *Earth in Mind*, the best ecological decisions come from our connection to place. Those that are literally grounded in the soil are the best for behaving within the limitations of that place. The United States is dominated by religious stories that are not of this place.

These dominant non-indigenous religions still encourage outmoded expansionist views and focus worshippers on the past. Traditions are highly valued and the future is just the place where grandchildren get to repeat them. Today's reality demands a radically different narrative. With 7.2 billion people, human needs and wants exceed nature's ability to provide, no matter how many prayers are chanted. The world's major religions reject this paradigm and create a cloak of sacred rituals around age-old beliefs. Organized religion holds immense political clout and does not want to lose that power through profound messaging changes. The mere suggestion that doctrine change is often treated as an act of blasphemy.

The Union of Concerned Scientists issued its Warning to Humanity appeal in 1992. Written and spearheaded by the late Henry Way Kendall, former UCS board chair, he spelled out a dire forecast for our ability to live on Earth unless we change our ways. This appeal did not grab our collective attention because science is not society's primary story. Our life-supporting planet is threatened by human numbers and modern lifestyles. Faith communities need to embrace this critically important idea. Until that happens, a story of living within our carrying capacity cannot and will not emerge unless society abandons faith all together and continues to embrace a secular world view.

Religion so often goes unquestioned. It is next to impossible to challenge someone's faith or sacred texts, yet so much of how we engage on challenging issues like overpopulation depends on the assumptions we make about the world. Even if people do not attend church regularly, their assumptions about the way the world works come from their upbringing. In general, non-indigenous religions put humans at the pinnacle of creation. We are the icing on the cake of a long line of organisms and our lives are dedicated to the betterment of our fellow humans. Overpopulation challenges that story. It says that we have been too successful and need to start trimming our numbers so that we don't run out of resources. It is difficult to reconcile these two ways of looking at humankind, and more often than not overpopulation is dismissed.

I graduated with an education doctorate in critical pedagogy in 2002. My doctoral program was made up of a cohort of racially diverse people dedicated to the purpose of promoting social justice through critical thinking. We discussed the need to dismantle racism and classism and read many texts about the struggles of feminism. We learned to apply critical thinking skills to everything but religion. Religion and its role in these topics were never questioned, perhaps because this program was housed in a Catholic university.

The Catholic Church is often the first religion one thinks of when naming adversaries of overpopulation. It is not alone. Most religions at their fundamental level oppose any doctrine that results in reduced family size. Their political strength and economic health is dependent upon large families. They see it as a matter of their faith's survival. It is very difficult for them to look further down the road and see that no one will survive if we destroy our planet's ability to support us. The Catholic Church is a very powerful political force especially in the developing world. They would like to be considered an advocate of human rights, and they do some commendable work in that arena. Instead, by advocating that birth control is against their religion, they are guilty of promoting more misery and suffering. Albert Einstein once said:

> I am convinced that some political and social activities and practices of the Catholic organizations are detrimental and even dangerous for the community as a whole, here and everywhere. I mention here only the fight against birth control at a time when

overpopulation in various countries has become a serious threat to the health of people and a grave obstacle to any attempt to organize peace on this planet.

The Philippines today is an example of what Einstein was talking about. This impoverished nation had 96 million people living on its 7,107 islands in 2013. If nothing dramatically changes, they are projected to reach 155 million by mid-century. Birth control is too expensive for the poorest slum-dwelling people of this mainly Catholic country. For many years there was a de facto ban on public access to birth control. Thankfully, activists in the Philippines have succeeded in their 14-year-long quest to bring free access to birth control to poor families. They fought the powerful Catholic Church saying that the law is necessary to stem population growth, reduce maternal death rates and help avoid unwanted pregnancies among poor women. They also say that making birth control available to the poor could help slow down the spread of sexually transmitted diseases, including HIV/ AIDS, which was on the rise in rural areas. The Catholic Church is fighting the law all the way to their Supreme Court. They still uphold the idea that poverty is caused by lack of jobs, not too many people. They are holding on to their story in spite of all of the evidence to the contrary.

Religious leaders mired in the past and their own survival have to undergo a radical transformation. They need to be concerned more about this world and let go of their focus on the next life. John Lennon asked us to imagine there is no heaven. That would be a great goal because the whole concept of going somewhere else can have the side effect of absolving us from the more pressing obligation to take care of this world and all of its natural resources and inhabitants. It is long overdue to get our spiritual and moral stories in line with the ecological realities of this fragile planet.

If we want to have a future on this living planet, all organized religions must change their story and promote a reverence for what science is revealing. A paradigm shift is required. Daniel Quinn reminds us in *Ishmael* that the knowledge of how to live on the Earth was known for countless generations by indigenous people before what he calls "totalitarian agriculture" was invented about 10,000 years ago. His gorilla protagonist says, "Given a story to enact that puts them [Humans] in accord with the world, they will live in accord with the world. But given a story to enact that puts them at odds with the world, as yours does, they will live at odds with the world. Given a story to enact in which they are the lords of the world, they will ACT like lords of the world."

We need a clarion call for all organized religions and faith communities to quit living at odds with the world and embrace overpopulation as a deeply moral issue. This narrative fits perfectly into the existing desire to prevent misery and suffering. If I am right and religion is more of an obstacle than a gateway to clear thinking on this issue, then the growing numbers of people who are living a secular life can only be good news. The growing secularization in America is a refreshing trend that allows for more critical thinking even as it has inspired a backlash of religiosity. One thing is certain: Overpopulation renders all religions irrelevant in the end because no one will be attending temples, mosques, churches or powwows on a planet void of us.

Chapter 8

The Whole Hot Truth

Overpopulation is one of the greatest threats to
human nature.

—Joe Rogan

Climate change activists deserve a chapter of their own for side-stepping overpopulation while supposedly saving us from climate disaster. They have done a stellar job making this frightening issue a part of everyday conversation in America, but have failed miserably in helping people understand how it is connected to overpopulation. It is absolutely stunning that these activists ignore the population issue.

The United Nations Population Fund reports that, "Each birth results not only in the emissions attributable to that person in his or her lifetime, but also the emissions of all his or her descendants. Hence, the emission savings from intended or planned births multiply with time."

Deadlock is typical at international climate change conferences, and it's mainly based on arguments between industrialized and developing countries about who will pay the costs of rising oceans, increasingly violent storms, dramatic weather changes, altered growing seasons, desertification, ocean acidification, and other issues. Even if all of this is resolved, the overpopulation issue will not allow for long-term success.

Fresh Energy, a nonprofit in the upper Midwest, claims it is leading the way to a clean energy future. I say they are not. They claim to be all about promoting greener technologies for getting our energy needs met. But they are technological Pollyannas. They do a great job informing people about how much carbon each of us in the United States contributes on average to global climate change each year. They conveniently forget to multiply 12,000–15,000 pounds of carbon per person per year by the total number of people in our country. Certainly we can lower that number with government support and incentives, but without multiplying that figure by the over 320 million we have and the three million added to the U.S. each year, we are clinging to false hopes and fuzzy math. Without accounting for our collective numbers, we are just hamsters on a wheel thinking we are doing something when all our efforts are being negated by population increases.

Climate change deniers have unforgivably poisoned this dialogue with anti-science based doubt. In response, climate change folks have circled their wagons and focused on climate change data and satellite photos to prove they are right. These dedicated leaders have overlooked the overpopulation issue to focus on facts related to climate change. Unfortunately, one of its driving factors was left in the dust.

Visiting any of their websites reveals a lot of talk about carbon and carbon offsets. They give the false impression that the problem of a warming planet can be solved solely with green technology and conservation measures. Just google "global warming facts" and you will get a list of 50 things you can do to help on this issue. Choosing to have a small family did not make the list.

Climate change activists have the microphone, but do not educate their growing audiences about the irrefutable connection to overpopulation. They leave the impression that climate change can be solved with biofuels, organic food, electric cars and solar panels, when each day the impact of population growth alone undermines those downstream acts.

Those who put all their eggs in the renewable energy basket do not account for the non-renewable minerals required for the great transition to solar, wind, and geothermal. Renewables are not the silver bullet we would like them to be, especially when the renewable energy requirement to replace fossil fuels increases with every new passenger added to Planet Earth.

Kurt Cobb, author of the eco-thriller *Prelude*, wrote in the October 1, 2010, *Christian Science Monitor* that:

> Perhaps the most important thing that people don't realize about building a renewable energy infrastructure is that most of the energy for building it will have to come from fossil fuels.

> Currently, 84 percent of all the energy consumed worldwide is produced using fossil fuels—oil, natural gas and coal . . . . This is what's been dubbed the rate-of-conversion problem. In a nutshell, is our rate of conversion away from fossil fuels fast enough

so as to avoid an unexpected drop in total energy available to society? Will we be far enough along in that conversion when fossil fuel supplies begin to decline so that we won't be forced into an energy austerity that could undermine the stability of our society?

The answer can't be known. But the numbers are not reassuring. Based on data from the U.S. Energy Information Administration, it would take more than 70 years to replace the world's current electrical generating capacity with renewables including hydro-electric, wind, solar, tidal, wave, geothermal, biomass and waste at the rate of installation seen from 2005 through 2009, the last years for which such data is available. And, that's if worldwide generating capacity—which has been expanding at a 4 percent clip per year—is instead held steady.

We are expanding because of population growth. This is how human numbers impact energy demand and the resulting effects of climate change. To claim that industry is solely to blame for the rising temperature of the atmosphere is ignoring a huge part of the equation.

To his credit, former Vice President Al Gore began this conversation in the film *An Inconvenient Truth*, but has since unhitched his wagon from the overpopulation train. He has gone so far as to deny that it's actually a big problem anymore and said that the problem is taking care of itself. The real tragedy is that he said this on *Late Night with David Letterman*. Millions watched and heard the wrong message. Every time he writes a book, he gets lots of press. Gore's latest book is *The Future: The Six Drivers of Global Change*. Population is listed as one of the drivers of global change, but he predicts global population will level off at 10 billion and this gruesome fact does not seem to trouble him much. Gore passes on the opportunity to inform his readers about how we don't need to assume this added growth. He could and should have said that we can and must avoid it.

The website www.world.org lists 100 top climate change websites. Overpopulation is not mentioned on any of them, not even once. Bill McKibben, who authored *Maybe One: A Personal and Environmental Argument* about the population issue, totally left out this part of the conversation on his 2012 Do the Math 350.org tour. Apparently doing the math doesn't include counting the number of humans contributing to our overall carbon footprint.

As my fellow overpopulation activists like to say, the Earth doesn't care how much carbon we put into the atmosphere as individuals. It cares what we do collectively. I know that the 90 or so corporations mainly responsible for climate change gases have been unscrupulous in how they have avoided cleaning up their industries. I abhor their planet-killing actions but have stopped attending climate change lectures because human numbers are not mentioned as a critical part of the solution. We must put pressure on these groups to tell the whole truth or they will not get our money.

Chapter 9

Know this Peace

The raging monster upon the land is population growth. In its presence, sustainability is but a fragile theoretical concept.

—Edward O. Wilson

I was once the vice president of World Citizen Inc., a wonderful organization dedicated to putting up Peace Poles in gardens and schools around the country. They also put on an amazing peace conference every year and invite the previous year's Nobel Peace Prize winner to attend. The leader and founder of this group, Lynn Elling, is a World War II veteran who really did get the population part of peace, but few peace organizations do.

A just peace is always the goal of progressives. But it is never possible when resources are scarce. Many predict that the next war will be fought over water. We talk about water scarcity but not about why water is scarce. Again, it's a simple equation. When too many people need water, you run out of water. Water is only renewable when it has time to recharge.

Justice goes out the window when resources are even perceived to be scarce. The pattern has been repeated for centuries. Demonize the enemy and steal their resources but not before abusing their citizens. This is exacerbated by overpopulation and it is impossible to have long-lasting peace without working toward sustainable population levels.

If one peruses the websites of Amnesty International, or any number of other peace and justice groups, there is no message about what rising population is doing to their cause. Amnesty International has a great slogan: Action for Human Rights, Hope for Humanity. I would suggest that there is little hope for humanity if we do not address over-population. Overpopulation makes it difficult to address individual concerns in a sea of people. People become anonymous in masses of humanity and massive suffering results.

There are many cities in overpopulated India where people die in the streets and are not dealt with for days. India is set to surpass China's population by 2025 if nothing is done to stop that horrific scenario. It is already a country with 17.5% of the world's population struggling to survive on 2.5% of the world's land. Many cultural taboos need to be overcome, including the pressure for women to produce sons. But there is only suffering in the forecast no matter how much money we send to peace and justice organizations unless there is a strong collective voice that attaches peace and justice to addressing overpopulation.

Egypt is another sobering example. The 1992 UN Cairo conference was a global effort to address the population issue. Since then, Egypt has gained 19 million people in a country that is nearly all desert. Its recent uprisings were sparked by a rise in food prices. During the Arab Spring, protesters blamed their government for not providing enough food or economic security to its ever growing population. While its government is riddled with problems, overpopulation, which created the imbalance in the first place, is rarely blamed as a culprit.

Look at the countries which are experiencing upheavals through the lens of overpopulation. You will find over and over again that genocide, poverty, war and strife are more prevalent in overpopulated places. Overpopulation always makes matters worse and unsolvable in the long term. Egypt cannot feed its 85 million people today and, if nothing is done, its population will grow to 105 million in the next 15 years. Bad leadership will probably be blamed for the suffering, but overpopulation will be the real culprit.

According to Robert Walker of the Population Institute,

> There is, in fact, an alarming correlation between failing states, countries with rapid population growth, and those with severe hunger. Many failing countries are heavily dependent upon external food aid for their survival. The UN's World Food Programme (WFP) is currently helping to feed one out of four Somalis, but Somalia's population is expected to jump by more than 150 percent in the next four decades. The Global Hunger Index lists the current situation in Niger as "extremely alarming," but Niger's population is expected to triple in the next 40 years.

In other words it is like a cat chasing its tail. One can never catch up with hunger when numbers keep rapidly increasing.

Bread for the World is an NGO that claims that it can end hunger in our lifetime, if everyone just did their part to focus on poverty and injustice. They completely live downstream and can't see the impossibility of that well-intended idea, because 9,000 people are being added to their bread lines every hour, net gain.

I want to live in a non-violent world. Organizations like Pathways to Peace say that peace is through environment but only in a spiritual way. They believe we must live lives that are spiritually connected to nature. They promote living non-violent lives and practicing compassion but do not fundamentally understand the dark force of overpopulation.

Writer, physicist, philosopher and anti-globalization activist Vandana Shiva is a hard person to criticize. She stands for so many of the issues I care about, from fighting corporate ownership and genetically modified seeds to promoting women's rights. She is an incredible person. Unfortunately she rates local control of resources as a priority over the issue of birthrates. She argues about the rights of local people to have ownership over their own natural resources and argues that corporations or governments should not control them. I have listened to many of her speeches, yet have never heard her even mention India's death march toward being the most overpopulated country in the world. She did raise the alarm about an incident in her native state Kerala, however. Coca-Cola took over and built a plant whose production consumed water to the tune of 1.5 million liters a day, causing a water shortage in a place with more than adequate rainfall. While corporations like Coca Cola are to blame for much ecological and societal damage, even with stellar corporate responsibility, overpopulation in India is condemning people to a desperate future.

I hope that she will continue to champion the rights of indigenous people against corporate greed while acknowledging that local people must not overpopulate their resources even if they get control of them again.

Imagine if all of the myriad of peacemakers around the world also understood the overpopulation issue and worked on it. Indeed, it would be a more peaceful world without scarcity driving so much of the distress that inevitably leads to injustice and war.

Chapter 10

Broken Microphones

News is something someone wants suppressed.
Everything else is just advertising.

—Lord Northcliffe

While many blame poor education programs on the lack of alarm over the overpopulation issue, the news is even more culpable. People do not read a lot of academic literature, but they do get a daily dose of news whether it is from cable TV or social media, newspapers or major news stations. They hear about wars, poverty, murders, and crop losses, but do not hear about overpopulation due to the nearly complete avoidance of this topic in the media.

In *Tradeoffs: Imperatives of Choice in a High-Tech World,* Edward Wenk, Jr. said, "Whatever literacy in science and technology the general public has reached is not from formal education. Rather, it is from the mass media. That responsibility of the press has been almost completely ignored."

In their book, *Hidden Agendas, How Journalists Influence the News* (2003), Lydia Miljan and Barry Cooper point to the power and influence journalists have because they can persuade their audiences to adopt their perspective. Their personal level of awareness and belief system strongly affects how they cover stories. What they know about and care about affect how they frame issues and ask questions. Judging from how few journalists bring up the overpopulation issue, it is not on their radar. Opportunities to bring up overpopulation come up in news stories all the time. Stories of scarcity and climate change are in the news every day. Yet rarely are journalists asking questions that would create an informed dialogue around the way overpopulation drives these problems.

I wish I could attribute the lack of coverage on this issue to the fact that so much of the media is now owned and operated by multinational, self-serving corporations. They are certainly a big part of it, but that does not account for the way the remaining independent journalists ignore this issue.

A journalist well-informed about the overpopulation crisis might ask, "How many people can our planet support and at what lifestyle and for how long?" I have yet to hear a journalist ask these in-depth questions while showing us a melting glacier or islands threatened with rising oceans. It would be wonderful to hear journalists ask, "Which of our raw materials that build our modern world are we running out of and how does the rate of growth impact that scarcity?" "When the deeper well is dug, how long before it too runs completely dry with a growing population?"

Amy Goodman of Democracy Now, La Pacifica Radio and the War and Peace Report is a hero of mine on so many issues. She has said, "Journalism is the only profession explicitly protected by the US Constitution because journalists are supposed to be the checks and balances on government. We are supposed to be holding those in power accountable. We are not supposed to be their megaphone. That's what corporate media have become." There are few journalists, like the very honorable Ms. Goodman, who are holding anyone accountable on the overpopulation issue. She is not afraid to ask tough questions, but I have yet to hear her ask a question in a war-torn country about its ability to sustain growing numbers of people and how that impacts the taking up of arms. Goodman and her ilk view overpopulation as another way of the rich telling the poor what to do. Progressive journalists do not seem to understand that the poor are the first victims of overpopulation. They have an obvious blind spot on this issue. It isn't about telling poor people how to live. It's about permitting them to live in numbers that can be sustained locally.

Haiti is a stunning example of this. The deforestation of this small mountainous island country of 10,714 square miles is due to its overpopulation, which has led to such serious soil erosion that a ring of mud surrounds their impoverished island. That mud was topsoil which could have grown food. This is not the perspective one hears even and especially from the left-leaning press. The sheer numbers of people who populate the Haitian landscape create slums where farms would otherwise be. One of the main reasons Haiti is unable to plant enough food for its own people is due to its overwhelming numbers. Foreign aid and church groups pour into the country all seeking to end Haiti's misery. Journalists cover stories of self-sacrificing good

Samaritans who are providing building materials for schools and sending a plethora of mattresses, food and pencils. They are not sending in the much needed forces of public health workers and social workers to help them reduce their overpopulation.

More journalists need to see the deeper sides of this issue. It's about viewing their stories through the lens of overpopulation and then being unafraid to report the truth. When a country is overpopulated, the poor end up living in the most environmentally vulnerable steep hillsides and in the bottom of valleys. It's astonishing that journalists covering the perpetual disasters in Bangladesh rarely reveal the simple fact that Bangladesh has 155 million inhabitants existing in a country the size of Wisconsin. This context would reveal a truth rarely heard from the media.

In 1991 I was very fortunate to be selected to take three young people to World Environment Day at the United Nations. Bill Moyers and John Denver spoke. Afterwards there was time to meet one of them and I chose my favorite journalist. We talked about the value of public television. Bill Moyers is unafraid to take on corporations and Tea Party Republicans. He gives a platform to those who do not otherwise get to share their stories about controversial issues. But, with the exception of his interview with Isaac Asimov years ago, he is not focusing his microphone on overpopulation at all. Just recently I met him again and personally gave him information on this issue. I now know that information about overpopulation is not the problem. The avoidance comes from a deeper place. In Moyers's case it could be that his Southern Baptist background is clouding his ability to see this issue, or it could be that he thinks of it as an oppressive issue to the most vulnerable among us. The ghosts of population control haunt this issue. The idea of governments telling people how many children to have often prevent the progressive journalists like Moyers from covering this topic.

The relatively few who are tackling this need to be mentioned. Author and columnist Paul Farrell of Market Watch has written boldly about the overpopulation issue. If you do a search on the Internet for Paul Farrell and overpopulation, you get six major articles that he has written. He is very frustrated that we do not connect this issue to our economic problems. It is so inspiring and encouraging that no matter what he is discussing, he brings up our overpopulation problem and how it is driving all of our other problems.

Ken Weiss covers environment and science issues for the Los Angeles Times. He has done a number of good articles on overpopulation and keeps his readers aware of this issue.

Julia Whitty is an environmental correspondent for Mother Jones magazine. She continues to be very good at reporting on it, particularly focusing on the conspiracy of silence that hovers over this issue from both the right and the left.

Gary Peters, a retired geology professor, writes about population with titles like, "Population Growth is Still the Biggest Problem Facing Humanity". Other bloggers like Ben Silva have also tried to enlighten with their postings on the threat to the world that overpopulation represents.

Southern California journalist Mark Cromer writes frequently about immigration and population issues. He was interviewed in Dave Gardner's Growthbusters film, as was Lisa Hymas, senior editor of Grist magazine. Lisa writes boldly about overpopulation as well.

Rex Weyler is a journalist, blogger and ecologist who is not afraid to cover the destruction left in the wake of human population pressure.

Alex Smith is a journalist, researcher and founder of Eco-shock Radio. In January of 2013 he interviewed Dr. Paul Erhlich with a refreshing intelligence indicating that he had done his homework on the issue. Unfortunately, he has a tiny following and needs support to keep his downloadable interviews going.

We need more journalists like these to ask the right questions and put this issue on the dinner plates of those watching the news. What if all the highly acclaimed mainstream journalists understood the crisis of overpopulation and reported on the news through this lens? It is crucially important for all journalists to treat overpopulation as an issue that permeates nearly every issue they cover. All of a sudden, traffic, violence, rising oil prices and violent storms would appear in a new light. To be sure, journalists compete with billions of dollars in advertising by corporations that tell Americans in 30-second sound bites not to worry because they are discovering more oil and gas reserves all the time. They compete with cable television shows that make entertainment out of litter-size families. Yet there is no counterpunch to the lies of omission people are absorbing during the 24/7 news cycle. Journalists and news organizations are always looking for a scoop. Here's one: Why are so few with the microphone deeply and responsibly informing audiences about overpopulation?

Imagine reporting on a building that exploded and the reporter asked if anyone died and how much damage was caused but never asked why the building exploded. That is what most journalists do with this issue. They leave it on the cutting room floor.

When reporters covered the 2004 tsunami that hit Sri Lanka and Sumatra, they covered the misery and suffering well. They did not state that the area was already so overpopulated that the poorest of its citizens were disproportionately killed because they were forced to set up their homesteads on the most marginal lands.

Journalists hold an important key to illuminating our worldview on this issue. They must do a better job than asking, "What's wrong with the population?" as Charlie Rose did when Ted Turner so rightly said on his show that population was directly connected to climate change.

A well-informed journalist would say something like this: "We are growing by 9,000 people per hour, last year we added over 70 million people to our warming planet, so how can educating each individual to turn off unnecessary lights possibly make any real contribution to reducing our total carbon footprint without humanely reducing the overall demand?"

At the end this book is an example of a letter we should all write to our favorite journalist and help them to start reporting on overpopulation as the most critical and overlooked issue of our time.

Chapter 11

Artists to the Rescue

Corporations fear the artist, who with the stroke of
a brush, the click of a shutter, the quip of a pen can
make the world upon which they depend, irrelevant.

—Steve Geske

Artists who are in a position to influence the world include comedians, filmmakers, dancers, musicians and poets as well as visual artists. They have a set of amazing tools which can provoke change in the world. "'Now that you have seen it you must act on it,' is the assumption of political art," says author and speaker Stephen Duncombe. Artists are gifted at creating a vision for something that has never existed before. They help us to grow to new places and see things that have never been seen before. As out-of-the-box thinkers, they push boundaries. They are unafraid to be bold and in doing so, they stimulate and provoke us to reconsidering life's current realities.

They encourage thinking and don't mind when the art lover in a museum brings their own interpretation to a piece. They invite ambiguity in a way that makes many activists bristle. Their subtle nature is a welcome approach to this issue because being straightforward and factual often invites backlash and denial.

In the visual artist's world, *Guernica* by Pablo Picasso is the quintessential political mural. It is all about the horror inflicted on innocent Spanish villagers in the Spanish Civil War. It was so political that Picasso said it could not be displayed in Spain until liberty and democracy had been restored to the area. When Guernica did go on display in September of 1981, it was displayed behind bomb-proof glass.

Diego Rivera was a muralist who saw his art as an important way to champion the rights of the working class and expose their exploitation. His work was so radical that he took to carrying a gun while he worked for self protection.

Contemporary artist Elin O'Hara Slavick, professor of visual art theory and practice at the University of North Carolina, used her art to express her anti-war views in a collection called *After Hiroshima*. There is a huge potential for visual artists to help society grasp over-population, but they first have to understand why it matters.

When corporate media took over the 24-hour news cycle, they limited open dialogue. News became controlled and often agenda driven. With the snap of his articulately sarcastic tongue HBO's John Oliver enlightens viewers about issues of the day the mainstream news media is missing. Comedians are a special kind of artist who opens our eyes with laughter. By using their multimedia talents to get our attention, they appeal to our emotional side. They get us excited about issues by tickling our funny bone with the day's ironic incidents. They bring us perspectives we are not hearing from mainstream media. They do a tremendous service to democracy.

Comedians have helped us to see the ridiculous side of our nature. Doug Stanhope takes a provocative look at our overpopulated world in his (albeit raunchy) bit called, "Abortion is Green". George Carlin was never afraid to be irreverent and included overpopulation in his repertoire. If more comedians did, we'd reach a lot of more mainstream people. Bill Maher has been bold in covering overpopulation too. He has interviewed Alan Weisman, award-winning author of *Countdown, the Last Great Hope for Mankind on Earth*. What if late night popular comedian/hosts like the iconic John Oliver and Larry Wilmore and their comedy writers took a stand on the overpopulation issue? Imagine how they could put newsmakers on the hot seat for ignoring our overpopulation crisis. Millions would be exposed to this issue in thirty minutes or less. It could go viral on social media and would trump anything overpopulation activists have been able to accomplish thus far.

Filmmakers are heroic for trying to raise our awareness about suffering in the world. They often do this at great risk to themselves. Unfortunately, most do this without making a case for the driving issue of overpopulation. One example is Kim Nguyen's film, *Children of Congo: From War to Witches*. It is about the suffering of children who are wars' most innocent victims. The filmmaker focused downstream on the hardships of street children and the building of care centers, never connecting their misery to the larger picture of overpopulation. How much more relevant this film would be if it told the story behind the misery: That the average number of children per woman is six and that the Democratic Republic of Congo has a huge overpopulation problem with a growth rate of 2.6 percent in a country which is already the fourth most populous in all of Africa. It would be a much more comprehensive documentary if it would have taken us upstream to look at overpopulation in this area of the world. Unless Congo changes their course, nearly 70 million people are set to double in 22 years, setting the stage for perpetual misery and war.

I have seen all of Michael Moore's movies and have all of his books, and met him right before *Bowling for Columbine* came out. He is a passionate filmmaker and can take credit for raising awareness on many important issues. Unfortunately, overpopulation isn't one of them yet.

Avatar was a very successful film. Director James Cameron packed a powerfully important message into the film's amazing animation, telling viewers that indigenous people protect our connection to Mother Nature. His tale got us to cheer for those who protect their resources with their stories and actions. But this 300+ million dollar film fell short of telling how colonialism is inspired by overpopulation.

There are so many examples like this that it is easier to illustrate the courageous artists among us. Writer Daniel Quinn uses his gift for writing fiction to teach us about what we are doing to the planet. Using a gorilla as his protagonist, his *Ishmael* series offers the reader a unique message. Ishmael teaches that we are acting in the modern world as if we don't need to pay attention to its natural systems. Quinn challenges the "Find more food to feed more people" paradigm. Quinn says that by feeding more people, you make things worse by interfering with the natural checks and balances of living systems. His books have been controversial because he is telling people what they don't want to hear, that humans are subject to the same natural laws of all other living species.

Actress Alexandra Paul has filmed a TEDx talk on her commitment to this issue. She tells of her own choice to be child-free in a world that is on a deadly exponential growth curve. When artists stand up and speak about an issue they can open up the eyes of their fans like no other type of leader. Celebrity is the ticket to winning over audiences who are not already in the choir. In a world plagued with political correctness, artists are given more cultural space to get their message across. I applaud the brave few who have made efforts to attract our attention on the overpopulation issue.

Another great example is the award-winning film *Growthbusters: Hooked on Growth* by filmmaker and activist Dave Gardner. In his film, Gardner interviews many environmental experts. Citizen-

Powered Media, his NGO, says that Dave will "film to save the planet." He mixes humorous stabs at pop culture with in-depth interviews as a way to get more people to wrap their heads around our overpopulation-inspired addiction to growth.

I have become friends with artist and curator John Schuerman in my hometown of Minneapolis. John is very concerned about overpopulation and is interested in using art as a medium for opening up a dialogue on this topic. He is the curator of an art show called, "Fruitful and Multiplying the Overpopulation Show," which toured in 2014. John believes that this kind of action will attract media and widen the discussion on this silenced issue.

Imagine the impact on our culture if a plethora of talented artists got this issue and tried to use their skills to open our eyes to its reality and potential. When journalists follow their lead by asking the tough questions, we will be well on our way to understanding and solving this curable problem.

Chapter 12

Politicians and Overpopulation
The Shortest Chapter

You can't negotiate with nature.

—Paul Erhlich

The 37th president of the United States, Richard M. Nixon, still holds the torch as the president who was the most alarmed about this issue. We currently have too much political polarization to expect that politicians will lead the charge on overpopulation. That wasn't always the case. In the 1960s population stabilization was a part of the national dialogue. Inspired by *The Population Bomb* by Paul Erhlich and an article by Garrett Hardin in the journal *Science* called, "The Tragedy of the Commons", President Richard Nixon sent a special message to Congress about population stabilization. Congress endorsed it.

In 1969, when the US population was 202.6 million, President Nixon said we need to "set forth a far-reaching commitment to limit population growth, and put in motion a broad range of government activities, both domestic and international." These activities included: (1) the creation of the Commission on Population Growth and the American Future; (2) increased research on birth-control methods of all types and the sociology of population growth; (3) expanded programs to train more people in the population and family planning fields, both in this country and abroad; (4) expanded research on the effects of population growth on our environment and on the world's food supply; and (5) increased domestic family planning assistance, aimed at providing adequate family planning services to all who want but cannot afford them. This was the beginning of the peak of American political will to deal with the problem.

Early in his presidency, President Obama was well-informed about the seriousness of overpopulation. He is also obviously painfully aware that the political climate is too tenuous for him to lead the way. This hurdle will only be overcome by a very extensive grassroots movement to demand leadership on the overpopulation crisis. Google "overpopulation and politicians" and you will come up empty. No politician in office or even out-of-office wants to touch this issue. Too many Americans remain unaware of how overpopulation is already impacting their lives. I have had private audiences with some of the more liberal politicians, but even when they admit it is a core issue, they'd rather play it safe and do their downstream work.

Most politicians today put their finger in the air and see which way the political winds are blowing. They also must follow the wishes of their major donors. It is so expensive to run campaigns that money talks louder than it should. Even the few remaining outspoken liberal senators and congressman are mute on this issue. Therefore when we look for leadership on this issue, we must look in the mirror! A grassroots movement, similar to the one that is taking on the gay marriage issue is what is needed. Because this issue is so politically volatile, politicians need to know that there is a groundswell of concern out there demanding their action.

There isn't a single congressman or woman who openly talks about this issue. Overpopulation gets conflated with two hot button issues, immigration and abortion, so they won't go anywhere near the population issue. Imagine a politician saying that the U.S. can no longer be a relief valve for other countries due to our own limited resources. Imagine them saying that because we are already over-pumping our aquifers, inviting more immigrants to live here is not even ethical. While that would be honest, it would be political suicide for a political leader to even approach the problem in a country of overpopulation illiteracy. Most people in the U.S. still believe in the motto written on the Statue of Liberty: "Give me your tired, your hungry, your poor," which should have had a clause in it that said, "Unless we are full and have reached the limits set forth by our natural resources."

Columnist Boris Johnson wrote for The Telegraph in 2007, "How the hell can we twitter on about tackling global warming, and reducing consumption, when we are continuing to add so relentlessly to the number of consumers? The answer is politics, and political cowardice." Politicians used to be the smartest people in the land but due to a number of factors, that is no longer the case.

So many of today's politicians are almost proud of the way they ignore science and its proven discoveries. Bill Nye, the Science Guy of public television fame, challenged Congressman Paul Broun from Georgia for claiming that being taught about evolution and the Big Bang theory was "all lies straight from the pit of hell." To quote the rest of this congressman's ignorant speech would give his myopic view of the world undeserved publicity. Nye so rightly said, "He is, by any measure, unqualified to make decisions about science, space, and technology." I would add that he has no basis for understanding the science behind overpopulation either, let alone the critical need to solve it.

In 2010, 52% of Congress did not believe in evolution. One can only imagine the fight Congress would put up to challenge the credibility of overpopulation if they are having misgivings about evolution.

The ironic thing is that democracy itself is threatened by overpopulation, the very thing political leaders are supposed to care about.

In an interview with Isaac Asimov in 1989, interviewer Bill Moyers asked, "What happens to the idea of the dignity of the human species if this population growth continues at its present rate?"

Asimov responded:

> It will be completely destroyed. I like to use what I call my bathroom metaphor: If two people live in an apartment and there are two bathrooms, then both have freedom of the bathroom. You can go to the bathroom any time you want to, stay as long as you want for whatever you need. And everyone believes in freedom of the bathroom; it should be right there in the Constitution. But if you have twenty people in the apartment and two bathrooms, no matter how much every person believes in freedom of the bathroom, there is no such thing. You have to set up time for each person, you have to bang on the door, "Aren't you through yet?" and so on.

Asimov concluded with the profound observation:

> In the same way, democracy cannot survive overpopulation. Human dignity cannot survive [overpopulation].Convenience and decency cannot survive [overpopulation]. As you put more and more people onto the world, the value of life not only declines—it disappears. It doesn't matter if someone dies, *the more people there are, the less one person matters.*

When I was in the sixth grade growing up in Minnesota, there were 2.3 million people and we had two senators. That means that each senator had roughly 1.15 million citizens to serve. Today we have 5.3 million people and still have only two senators. Each senator has to serve roughly 2.1 million. Our democracy has been weakened by overpopulation yet political leaders are ironically the last to discuss this issue.

Chapter 13

Like Herding Cats
Population Groups to the Rescue?

The human overpopulation issue is the topic I
see as the most vital to solve if our children and
grandchildren are to have a good quality of life.

—Alexandra Paul

I wish I could report that all of the population NGOs are working together in a coordinated effort. It would be productive to have one clear
message teaching people that the world is overpopulated relative to the
planet's limited and quickly diminishing resources. How wonderful it
would be to collectively conclude that overpopulation is solvable and
promote that as a unified message?

Unfortunately, these groups could be more accurately described
as siblings who love each other but spend a lot of time quarrel-
ing. Some don't even come home for the holidays. They argue over
the best way to approach this crisis. Some have fallen prey to political correctness because working on this issue is so challenging.
Language is often changed as they try to tiptoe though this issue
without alarming their current and potential funders. The focus
of these groups varies, which makes it even more difficult to agree
on a single message. Some population groups focus strictly on the
U.S. population while others focus on world population. Some
groups offer solutions which are dramatic while others just inform.

Many population groups disagree about even using the word
"*over*population" for fear it will raise eyebrows and turn people away.
I once challenged a woman from a population group in England who
said they did not dare use the word "*over*population". I asked her when
it was going to be okay to tell people the whole truth.

It is more popular among population groups to educate about the problem of population 'growth'. They offer solutions that address the 73 million added passengers to Planet Earth each year. Only a handful of groups promote the message that we are *over*populated and must focus on humanely reducing our numbers to a sustainable level through voluntary one-child policies.

Each group has a piece of the pie, but the pie comes in too many flavors for the general public or our leaders to get a clear, direct message. Because the road to understanding this issue is laden with political land mines, some approach it delicately, while others bulldoze ahead and suffer explosive reactions from those not ready to hear the sobering truth about the catastrophe we are facing. The land mines come from all directions, making each group ponder how best to avoid them without diluting their message.

Below is a brief delineation of just a few key players in the NGO world of population groups, highlighting each group's core message. The best scenario would be to create a well-funded coordinated global overpopulation education campaign. My vision is that all population groups come together with a crystal clear message that first explains the whole truth about overpopulation and resource scarcity then shines a light on how this is solvable by humanely scaling back our reproduction.

Citizen Powered Media/Growth Busters
- Core message: Uses film and other multimedia to counter the growth paradigm in our society.
- Website: growthbusters.org

Millennium Alliance for Humanity and the Biosphere
- Core message: Create a global network of social scientists, humanists, and scholars in related fields whose collective knowledge can be harnessed to support global civil society in shifting human cultures and institutions toward sustainable practices.
- Website: mahb.stanford.edu

Negative Population Growth (NPG)
- Core message: Reduce immigration and enforce small families to reduce U.S. population.
- Website: npg.org

Numbers USA
- Core message: The U.S. is overpopulated mostly due to mass immigration and we therefore must stop the flow of immigrants into the country.

- numbersusa.org

Population Connection
- Core message: Reduce global growth with family planning education.
- Website: populationconnection.org

Population Media Center
- Core message: Uses serialized dramas to bring about changes in attitudes within individual countries with sensitive material worldwide.
- Website: populationmedia.org

World Overpopulation Awareness
- Core message: The world is overpopulated due to both population numbers and consumption. Solutions proposed include lifestyle changes, women's empowerment.
- worldoverpopulation.org

World Population Balance
- Core message: Overpopulation is solvable. One-child families will bring about needed reduction in global population.
- Website: worldpopulationbalance.org

Chapter 14

Unsustainably Green

Unless we face world population head on we are
doing nothing more than sticking a Band-Aid on a
fast growing cancerous tumor.

—Dan Brown

There is no such thing as a sustainable act on an overpopulated planet. Doing anything, from buying greener technology to using reusable bags, cannot be sustained over time. So many groups call themselves sustainable, or have sustainability in their mission statements, but completely avoid the overpopulation issue. Human numbers are avoided and dismissed for a variety of reasons but clearly the amount of consumers matters even if it is politically unpopular to mention them.

The late Dr. Al Bartlett, professor emeritus in physics at University of Colorado Boulder, eloquently described our hypocritical definitions of sustainability in his writings and publications. He frequently pointed out that we must look at sustainability as an act that can be sustained over a long unspecified amount of time.

Wikipedia's definition of sustainability is a typical reflection of the way in which most people dance around the impact of human numbers. Their long-winded reference to the unlikely possibility that we can achieve sustainability ignores overpopulation. "Despite the increased popularity of the use of the term 'sustainability', the possibility that human societies will achieve environmental sustainability has been, and continues to be, questioned—in light of environmental degradation, climate change, overconsumption, and societies' pursuit of indefinite economic growth in a closed system."

Only using the word "overconsumption" to describe sustainability implies we can address using up the Earth's resources by focusing on individual behaviors and policy changes.

Chip and Dan Heath wrote the eye-opening book *Make it Stick: How to Make Change When Change is Hard*. To abbreviate their message, the Heaths used the metaphor of a rider on an elephant. The rider is the intellect, the elephant is the emotional self. The rider is on top of the elephant telling it what to do and must give clear direction to the elephant or else the emotional self spins out of control and goes off in irrational directions. When trying to make people change a behavior, we often overstimulate their intellect with information without giving them with clear direction what they should do about it. Without the proper direction to their 'elephant', they can't handle it so they deny and avoid the truth.

Our supposed allies on this issue are those who measure resources and changes in climate. These researchers document in detail how rapidly we are running out of everything essential by tracking fossil fuels, water supplies, fisheries, crop production and every resource we need to keep our lives going. Reading their meticulous work is terrifying. They leave their readers hanging. Because they don't say that in order to avoid the cliff of collapse we have to start having less than two children per couple, people become distraught and ineffective.

These bright, vital environmental bean counters advise us to tinker with the way we consume resources and encourage us to become individually resilient. This advice is grotesquely inadequate. It represents the expert-approved avoidance that has long plagued this issue. First, they say the world's population is growing exponentially and consuming limited resources, then they advise us to save water in our basements, become a organic growers and leave the electric grid. They don't tell us the harsh reality of being prepared in a world that is mostly unprepared for disaster. To be blunt, one had better be heavily armed. Hungry and thirsty people will stop at nothing to get what we have carefully stashed away.

What is puzzling is how well-informed people come up with such feeble conclusions after generating such alarming statistics. Lester Brown, of the Earth Policy Institute, past president of World Watch Institute and author of many books including, *Full Planet, Empty Plates: The New Geopolitics of Food Scarcity*, is one of them. He has stated countless sobering facts, including: "As a result of population growth, there will be scarcely one-fourth as much freshwater per person in 2050 as there is in the world today." Yet Brown and many others do not clearly and firmly advocate for global initiatives on humane population reduction. They give insufficient advice on minimizing the impact of the resource shortage crisis. They are not openly advocating for a concerted effort to humanely reduce population and that is a shame.

Al Gore is sounding the alarm on our planet's rapid warming, yet he focuses his solutions on the proliferation of electric cars. Kurt Dahl, who created The Population Elephant website, calls Al Gore, Lester Brown and freelance author Fred Pearce "the Grand Priests of False Hope." Dahl eloquently interprets their actions in this statement: "The world will increase in population by fifty percent over the next fifty years. Consequently, demand for everything will increase by a minimum of fifty percent. Understand this clearly—we will need fifty percent more food, fifty percent more fuel, water, clothing, shoes, and on and on. We will produce fifty percent more pollutants, sewage, greenhouse gases and on and on and on. No reasonable amount of 'Green' behavior changes could possibly compensate for this tsunami of demand generated by population growth. Just do the math. It's not possible."

Heather Rogers, author of *Green Gone Wrong,* agrees that we cannot save the world with a series of green products. She points out how corporations have corrupted efforts to reduce carbon footprints. Heather's advice is to convert industrialized farming to agroecology, a holistic method of farming. Proponents of this system claim they can double productivity of organic produce while protecting soils and rivers. Rogers is ignoring the fact that population growth will require more and more productivity in order to keep up with demand and sustainability will never be reached.

It is frustrating to hear about a global crisis followed by feeble recommendations. Best-selling author Thomas Friedman personifies this phenomenon. In *Hot, Flat and Crowded* Friedman concludes that we must embrace green technology to wiggle our way out of climate change. Friedman joins a lengthy list of writers shirking their duty by not fully informing their readers about what is really happening to our planet. They neglect, or even refuse, to reveal the whole truth that overpopulation and population growth prevent making long-term gains on carbon reduction with greener technology.

Thomas Friedman, Al Gore and Lester Brown are all brilliant. I am humbled by their prolific writing abilities, but I must hold their feet to the fire. Someone has to call out their blatant omission. People cannot begin to take appropriate actions if they do not know the full truth.

These people wield great political power. They have the microphone and are seen as experts on global issues. Their word is taken as gospel. When they gloss over and even skip the overpopulation issue, it makes it hard for those in the know to get any press at all. Though looking like environmental heroes, they are inadvertently condemning us to a dismal future. I am unsure if they are deliberately avoiding the facts or are completely unaware of the impact adding 9,000 people per hour has on our overpopulated planet.

In recent years, whenever Minnesota Public Radio reported on the environment, they called Dr. Jonathan Foley, the former director of the Institute on the Environment at the University of Minnesota. He was their go-to person and regularly presented his version of what is happening to our planet. He believes we can and must provide food to meet the demands of a growing population. Like Heather Rogers, he focuses his audiences' attention on technologies that can expand per acre yields. He doesn't think about the very real consequences of the additional population growth which will result from the success of feeding additional millions. Once there are more people even more food will need to be grown and the Earth will fail to provide for them at some point, thus creating an even greater catastrophe. Dr. Jonathan Foley has the appropriate credentials as an award-winning speaker and writer. The MPR interviewers are woefully uninformed on the overpopulation issue and look no further to explore this issue even though Dr. Foley is not really an overpopulation expert. Dr. Foley's lack of concern about overpopulation is based on the fact that the overall rate of population increase has decreased. This is true but irrelevant because slow growth on a seriously overpopulated planet is like drowning in 10 feet of water instead of 30 feet.

Dr. Foley is not the only false messiah in the media today. Dr. Hans Rosling is a very well-spoken public health expert who makes compelling videos about how we can all live in a better world in spite of our growing numbers. He speaks of a world which can handle billions more and promotes this delusion in a heartfelt way. The unsuspecting, uneducated world flocks to his message because it is a reassuring lie and feels better than hearing the whole honest truth about overpopulation.

Is giving half the story better than not saying anything at all? Is it good that at least the sustainability folks are telling people part of the truth? Is it okay that they discuss the realities of human-induced climate change even though they ignore the part about how many there are of us producing these gases? I have this argument with my friends and colleagues. Many say I should be happy that at least these activists alert people to globally troubling issues. I say it is like telling people to head for the lifeboats but sending them to the wrong side of the ship.

Nothing illustrates the story of half-truths better than the smart growth movement. The claim by many in the sustainability movement that growth has to be smart is countered beautifully by my late colleague Al Bartlett. He memorably commented, "Whether the growth is smart or dumb, the growth destroys the environment. "Growth management" is a favorite term used by planners and politicians. With planning, smart growth will destroy the environment, but it will do it in a sensitive way. It's like buying a ticket on the Titanic. You can be smart and go first class, or you can be dumb and go steerage. In both cases, the result is the same. But given the choice, most people would go first class."

Chapter 15

Trend Need Not be Destiny

Humanity cannot overcome the ills of
overpopulation Human dignity cannot survive it.
Convenience and decency cannot survive it.

—Isaac Asimov

Alon Tal, former visiting professor at the Stanford Center for Conservation Biology said, "The good news is that public policy matters and can reduce overpopulation. Many countries, from Bangladesh and Iran to Singapore and Thailand, adopted policies that incentify small families, make birth control available, provide better social security and most of all—empower women. The results are remarkable, showing that trend need not be destiny."

Note he did not place his hope on technology or better distribution of resources. He is telling the unadulterated truth, that hope lies in humanely reducing births. Activists frequently tell me they would rather work on an issue that has a chance for success. Without addressing overpopulation, their work on all other downstream issues will ultimately fail. If they understood that, I believe they would join me upstream.

Overpopulation is the driver of the unsustainability problems we care about. Working downstream from that issue may be easier in the short term and currently more politically correct, but is ultimately very ineffective. I say "currently" politically correct because the cultural climate can change. It must change. While it is true that this issue is shunned now, it is not a permanent state. The smoking issue is a great example of how an issue can go from acceptable to unacceptable in a relatively short period of time with the right data and a well-crafted campaign. We can make dramatic changes in cultural perspectives.

Twenty-three years ago my health club had a smoking section in it. Just last year our nature center banned all outdoor smoking without a protest.

There are many wise and courageous people speaking out on this issue. In fact there are so many I cannot do them all justice in these pages. I do, however, wish they were more famous and better funded. I want to focus a spotlight on them so that we can all leave this book inspired to take on the task of steering our ship in the right direction.

Please look them up and read in depth about their credentials and the legacy they are building with their outspoken efforts. I have included some of their websites in the appendix.

Comprehensive population reduction with the desired effects of greater health and well being for all has already happened in the country of Thailand. The reason Thailand is mentioned frequently as a success story is due to the efforts and commitment of one very special man. He made a decision to help his country by first working on overpopulation. He was successful in leading a nationwide campaign beginning in the 1970s to demystify birth control, particularly condoms, and make them ubiquitous in his beloved country.

Thailand's Mechai Viravaidya, as mentioned earlier, did not let his country's modest Buddhist inclinations stop him from trying to make them comfortable with using condoms. He used his relative wealth to do his country a huge favor and help them get their population growth under control. He was very successful. Women on average were having seven children. With the encouragement, education, availability of birth control, and choices to prevent births, they did just that. They reduced that number to 1.5 on average. Mechai demonstrated that even in a typically shy, mostly Buddhist country, it can be done.

Dr. Al Bartlett, the late physics professor emeritus from the University of Colorado Boulder was a great leader on this issue. His well-organized lectures are now on YouTube and offer a step-by-step analysis about exponential growth. He begins his talk with this statement: "The greatest shortcoming of the human race is our inability to understand the exponential function." It is worth watching repeatedly so that we can focus on what matters, and stop idolizing growth in a finite space.

Jeremy Grantham is an economist and asset money manager who understands the overpopulation issue. He is the co-founder and chief investment strategist for Grantham Mayo Van Otterloo, which manages over $97 billion in assets. This economist has stated, "The world is in the midst of a great paradigm shift driven by explosive population growth and its corresponding pressure on natural resources."

Grantham is rare in the investment community in that he has generated a lot of discussion and attention to this issue. Commenting on an article about Grantham by Richard Brewer, author of *Conservancy: The Land Trust Movement in America*, Dick Klade said, "We can feed starving children in Somalia forever, and if we cannot somehow prevent the overproduction of children in Somalia, we accomplish nothing."

Sir David Attenborough, Britain's foremost natural history filmmaker, speaks up frequently on overpopulation. His journeys around the world have opened his eyes to the way species are being devastated by overpopulation. He declared, "We are a plague on the Earth. It's coming home to roost over the next 50 years or so. It's not just climate change; it's sheer space, places to grow food for this enormous horde. Either we limit our population growth or the natural world will do it for us, and the natural world is doing it for us right now."

Ted Turner is outspoken on this issue and has taken heat for it. He has spoken up on overpopulation during television interviews. "We're too many people; that's why we have global warming," he once told interviewer Charlie Rose. "Too many people are using too much stuff. On a voluntary basis, everybody in the world's got to pledge to themselves that one or two children is it." Back in 1997 he put his money where his heart is. He pledged one billion dollars to help the United Nations deal with population, environment and health.

Martin Luther King, Jr. is a hero to many on civil rights and on peace issues. He is also a hero on the overpopulation issue. If he had lived a full life, chances are he would have acted on his words quoted earlier as he received the Margaret Sanger Award for Human Rights in 1966.

Bruce Phillips is a science educator who uses film as a medium in which to raise awareness about the threat of overpopulation. "One Planet, One Child" is a powerful short video which tells the truth about our planet's future in a creatively palatable way.

Dick Smith is the author of *Dick Smith's Population Crisis: The Dangers of Unsustainable Growth for Australia*. He sounded the alarm for his fellow countrymen and women when he challenged, "There comes a time when continuing with perpetual growth in the use of resources and energy is more about greed than improving the quality of life." In an effort to bring media attention to the overpopulation issue, Dick offered a million dollars to someone under 30 if they could create a successful campaign to educate the world on this crisis.

There have not been a lot of women to quote on this issue, but Madeline Weld, president of the Population Institute Canada, is a courageously brilliant woman whom I have quoted many times in this book. She is an outspoken advocate for Canada to keep a stable population for its future. I have had the good fortune to get to know her in the last few years.

Trend need not be destiny because hope for the future lies in connecting population balance and reduction with the goals of the NGOs in the world. There are 1.5 million NGOs in the U.S., three million NGOs in India, 200,000 NGOs in Russia, and so on around the world. All of these organizations have a mission to bring food to the poor, peace to warfare-burdened countries, water to drought areas and cures for diseases. They have great missions to anyone with a heart. If all of these NGOs adjusted their mission and websites to include something like the following message, it would truly be a recipe for success:

> We want to save endangered species in South Africa, but we know that we won't be successful if we don't also contribute to the population organizations working in South Africa. They are trying to reduce the stresses caused by overpopulation with culturally sensitive population reduction programs. For every donation you make to our organization, 50% will go towards funding population groups and their efforts to bring the cultural expectation of family size down while providing free birth control in cities and rural communities.

Social psychologist Jonathan Haidt says that the only time we act uniformly as a species in one direction is when we can "circle around sacred values and principles". He goes on to say that we can depolarize our issues. We first must see a common threat that affects us all and then develop a common ground on which to resolve that threat. To begin to address our many problems, we must circle around the 'sacred' principle that overpopulation is undermining our ability to make long-term progress. Once we begin to see that without lowering population to sustainable levels we cannot move forward, we are more likely to jump on board. Enlightened leaders will do this out of an interest to further their own mission.

Many people are ecologically aware on some level. They know that something is wrong in terms of what we are asking the third planet from the sun to do for us. They are just not fully awake. Once awakened to our situation, it is my hope they will realize that telling the whole story is actually liberating. We know that whatever we are collectively doing it is not working and it's time to try something else.

New narratives can be constructed by promoting small families as a ticket to less misery and suffering in the world with more room for wildlife.

What this means for donors who get it

It can be powerful to refuse to give money to an organization that doesn't make a commitment to educate and work on the overpopulation issue, especially if many people do it. Next time Clean Water Action or Greenpeace call to ask for donations, ask what they are doing about the overpopulation issue. Frequently they say they are focused on their issue. That is a teachable moment. Tell them it's impossible to be successful in the long term unless we set out to solve the crisis of overpopulation.

Credo Mobile is a phone company dedicated to progressive issues. Credo asks its members to round up their bill and donate each month to a list of progressive organizations. I no longer round up my bill because, as of this writing, they have refused to add any population organization to their list, even after several requests.

What this means for the organizations themselves

NGOs must be courageous. They must wake up and discover that planting trees, recycling, carbon sequestering, wind turbines, solar panels and legalizing hemp growing will not save us in the absence of serious population reduction. They need to partner with population organizations, dedicate space on their website and in their brochures to show how rapidly we are running out of vital resources due to our growing billions. They need not abandon their missions, but they do need to take a long hard look at what their projects will really accomplish in the context of overpopulation.

Carbon Offsets to Alleviate Poverty (COTAP), Bill Clinton's organization, must fund culturally respectful ways to curb and reduce the population of Malawi so that the tree plantings have a chance to work. Matt Damon needs to work more upstream and help each country determine what its sustainable numbers are, then reach out to population groups. Water.org can do this while finding a means to get clean water to the people. Sean Penn must work with Haiti's leaders on the overpopulation issue to find ways in which to educate their leaders to get them on board to hold down and reduce Haiti's population.

Educating our Leaders on this Issue

John Lennon asked us to imagine a very different world than we have now. He wanted us to live in a world without war and injustice. It's unfortunate that even this insightful cultural icon and his wife Yoko Ono felt that overpopulation was a myth. They thought it was perpetrated by the government to distract us from other 'real' problems. When John and Yoko were interviewed by Dick Cavett they claimed there were enough resources to go around. They advocated for a balance between rich and poor. But now over 40 years later, we have over three billion additional passengers to a planet now suffering even more from drastic reductions in ocean fish, farmland, water and oil.

I have been on a long and lonely search for the right words that would convince activists why and how human numbers matter. The ability to ignore the overpopulation crisis demonstrates how ecologically out of touch even activists can be. Today Yoko Ono and her son Sean Lennon are activists once again, working to stop fracking for natural gas in New York. They rightly point out the dangers to our air, water and land that fracking causes. But they still do not discuss what is driving the need for more natural gas. To be sure, corporations see only dollar signs and are evil in the way they ignore pollution and the disrupted lives it creates. But we need to ask ourselves, what is driving the need for more energy? The toxic extraction of tar sands oil is economically fueled by increasing demand.

I am asking everyone to imagine a truly sustainable world, one with about 1.5 billion inhabitants, all ecologically literate. That is the number most experts say we could sustain if we got busy. However, the longer we wait, the less people will be able to live sustainably on Earth. Imagine a world where all of the caring celebrities, the human rights organizations, the conservation groups, the peace groups and the artists all took on overpopulation as their overarching message. I believe that the solutions would come pouring in and become quite transparent, especially if journalists got on board. When we finally realized that smoking was killing us, we passed legislation to make us healthier. When we finally understand that overpopulation drives all other major issues, we will develop policies that make more ecological sense.

To those who are aware but have given up any hope on this issue, I remind them that abolitionists probably heard the same arguments from those who believed slavery had no hope of ever ending. With two million slaves and nearly decades of horrific institutionalization, they had no reason to believe they would ever succeed. They just knew that slavery was morally wrong and caused the suffering of millions of human beings. They knew they could not stop even in the face of incredible odds.

If I focused on winning, I would lose my way. I would waste precious time doubting my effort to break through on this issue. So I focus on the journey. What matters is that I am on the right path, the one that has a chance of working. My goal is to help end the denial, the dodging and the backlash. I want to remove the luxury of ignorance from this issue, for it is a luxury to work on bettering the world without addressing overpopulation.

I am not advocating we stop doing downstream acts, just that we merge our efforts in order to become stronger and successful. I still compost, recycle, shop with cloth bags and grow an organic garden; it's just that I know that I must also advocate for truly sustainable populations at home and abroad in order to make a long-term difference.

Arguments about the probability of success on this issue occupy precious time that could be spent more productively. We need to imagine what the world would look like if all activists and the NGOs they support made overpopulation their top priority. In the movie *Dumb and Dumber,* Jim Carrey's character asks a pretty woman what his chances are of taking her on a date. To paraphrase, she answers, "One in a million." He responded with the most optimistic of answers. "You mean I have a chance?" He gets all excited about that possibility.

I am excited about the possibility of solving this issue, no matter what the odds. Overpopulation is solvable. This is not a whimsical statement. It is not solvable simply because we want it to be. It is already being solved in Thailand, Iran, Italy, Brazil, Mexico and a number of other countries. Religion does not have to be an obstacle as long as both leaders and followers understand that a new paradigm is upon us. Ancient edicts of promoting large families are the source of today's troubles and we must be brave enough to challenge those paradigms and rewrite the rules. If Iran can turn this around, then we need to be unafraid to take on the challenge in the West. When I start seeing, "One Child Families Can Save the World" at bus stops and billboards, I will know we have broken through the fog.

I hope I have made a case for the compassionate nature of this cause, for it has the potential of reducing so much misery, suffering and early death in the world. There is no easy road ahead, but the path I have carved out does have a light at the end of the tunnel. Humanely solving human overpopulation requires activists to have the courage to be aware, the vision to be hopeful and the fortitude to work hard on a seemingly impossible task. But to do anything less than helping people to understand this issue will not be a win for humanity. The time to embrace it is long overdue. I hope this book will inspire my fellow activists to get involved and help the world change course. I think preserving a livable planet is worth it.

Tick Tick Tick

Every second, the sound
of new passengers
added to our spaceship
long past being able to sustain them
Work at the problem's source
where the stream begins as just a trickle
Tick Tick Tick
It takes courage to work upstream
and stay there
when the world is pushing us
further down
to focus on cures
instead of causes
at results
instead of actions
Tick Tick Tick
It takes wisdom to know
that all will be futile
if we don't work at the source
and expose our futile paradigm
For possibility lives
and justice resides
when we start to get that numbers matter
that growth is the ideology
of a cancer cell
on a planet that was never limitless
except in ignorance
perhaps in creativity
Tick Tick Tick
Don't let them tell you
you don't have a heart because
you work upstream
for as the wizard had to show the Tinman
those who work upstream
have always had the biggest hearts of all.

—Karen I. Shragg

Bibliography

Books and Articles

Brewer, R. (2003). *Conservancy: The land trust movement in America.* Lebanon, NH: Dartmouth College.

Brown, L. (2012). *Full planet, empty plates: The new geopolitics of food scarcity.* New York: W. W. Norton & Company.

Catton, W. (1980). *Overshoot, the ecological basis of revolutionary change.* Urbana: University of Illinois.

Clugston, C. O. (2012). *Scarcity: Humanity's final chapter: The realities, choices and likely outcomes associated with ever-increasing nonrenewable natural resource scarcity.* Florida: Book Locker.

Cobb, K. (2010). *Prelude.* Portage, MI.: Public Interest Communication.

Ehrlich, P. (1968). *The population bomb.* New York: Ballantine Books.

Foreman, D. (2011). *Man swarm and the killing of wildlife.* Durango, CO: Raven's Eye Press.

Friedman, T. (2008). *Hot, flat, and crowded: Why we need a green revolution-- and how it can renew America.* New York: Farrar, Straus and Giroux.

Geske, S., & Hansen, H. (2011-12). *A survival guide for the enlightened leader.* Clearwater, MN: Healing Leaders.

Gore, A. (2012). *The future: Six drivers of global change.* New York: Random House Press.

Hardin, G. (1968, Dec 13). The tragedy of the commons. *Science,* 1243-1248. Retrieved from http://sciencemag.org

Heath, C., & Heath, D. (2010). *Switch: How to change things when change is hard.* New York: Crown Business.

Miljan, L., & Cooper, B. (2003). Hidden agendas: How journalists influence the news. Vancouver: UBC Press.

Iscol, J., & Cookson, P. (2012). *Hearts on fire: Stories of today's visionaries igniting idealism into action.* New York: Random House Trade Paperbacks.

Mumford, S. D. (2015, April). *In overcoming overpopulation: The rise and fall of American political will.* The Center for Research on Population and Security, 1994.

Orr, D. (1994). *Earth in mind: On education, environment, and the human prospect.* Washington, DC: Island Press.

Quinn, D. (2011). *Ishmael.* Bridgewater, NJ: Distributed by Paw Prints/ Baker & Taylor.

Rogers, H. (2010). *Green gone wrong: How our economy is undermining the environmental revolution.* New York: Scribner.

Smith, D. (2011). *Dick Smith's population crisis: The dangers of unsustainable growth for Australia.* Crows Nest, N.S.W.: Allen & Unwin.

Weisman, A. (2013). *Countdown: Our last, best hope for a future on earth?* New York: Little, Brown & Company.

Wenk, E. (1986). *Tradeoffs: Imperatives of choice in a high-tech world.* Baltimore: Johns Hopkins University Press.

White, L. (1967). *The historical roots of our ecological crisis.* Science. Retrieved from http://sciencemag.org.

Websites

Globalfootprintnetwork.org

Mahb.stanford.edu

Npg.org

Numbersusa.org

Oneplanetonechild.org

Populationconnection.org

Populationelephant.org

Populationinstitutecanada.ca

Populationmedia.org

Worldpopulationbalance.org

Worldoverpopulationbalance.org

Resources

All of the talks I conduct on this topic end with a question and answer session. One of the biggest critiques I have received over the years is that I don't leave people with something to do. Accepting a new fact-based narrative about what is really happening on our planet is hard to swallow, but those who begin to comprehend this issue immediately want to know what they can do about it. I have included this resource section in order to be sure that this book does not leave people without a clear direction for what they can do about the most challenging issue of our time.

Recommended Websites

worldpopulationbalance.org
growthbusters.org

Heroes Present and Past on the Overpopulation Issue

Don't just believe me, study the work and writings from the following heroes of the past and present.

Dr. Al Bartlett: The late professor emeritus of physics, University of Colorado Boulder. Author, *Laws Relating to Sustainability* and *The Essential Exponential!* Al died in 2013 but his lectures are still on YouTube and are a great resource.

Mark Cromer: Southern California journalist who writes frequently about immigration and population issues. He can be reached at mrcromer@aol.com.

Paul Ehrlich: Biologist, professor of population studies, Stanford University professor, author of *The Population Bomb* and *The Population Explosion,* co-author, *Humanity on a Tightrope.*

Paul Farrell: Columnist for Market Watch, writes frequently about overpopulation and doesn't have much time for activists who ignore this issue.

Dave Foreman: Author of *Man Swarm and the Killing of Wildlif.*

Dave Gardner: Filmmaker, founder of Citizen-Powered Media and producer/director/writer of *Growthbusters: Hooked on Growth.*

Garrett Hardin: American ecologist who lived from 1915–2003, author of *The Tragedy of the Commons.*

Lisa Hymas: Senior editor of Grist Magazine.

Chris Martenson: Author of *The Crash Course.*

Pete McCloskey: Former U.S. Representative, co-sponsor of the original Earth Day.

Dennis Meadows: Director of Club of Rome Project on the Predicament of Mankind, MIT 1970–1972.

Alexandra Paul: Actress, activist, speaker.

Dave Paxson: President and founder of World Population Balance.

Bruce Phillips: Video producer of One *Planet, One Child*, former biology instructor.

William Rees: Population ecologist professor at University of British Columbia, co-author of *Our Ecological Footprint.*

William Ryerson: Founder and president of Population Media Center.

Dick Smith: Founder of Dick Smith Electronics, author of *Dick Smith's Population Crisis.*

Madeline Weld: President of Population Institute of Canada.

Sample Letter to Journalists

Journalists often like to hear from their readers. Challenging their lack of coverage on this topic could be key to opening up this issue to the public for a better understanding of overpopulation. Of course the more people who do this the more chances there are of pressuring them to respond to a public demand for telling the whole truth. On the following page is a sample letter you can use to contact journalists regarding the critical issue of overpopulation.

I have selected you as a target for this request because I consider you to be professional journalists. A good journalist helps to uphold democracy. Without journalists like you, we have no hope of having a vital participatory democracy.

I have been following your career for years. The likely reason it is missing is: a) you are not aware of it and its impact on the issues you cover; b) you are somewhat afraid of the issue but as yet do not comprehend its vital role; or c) you are afraid to bring it up for fear of losing your job. So I am going to make a request that you do the homework on this issue like you would any other and include this framing in your reporting from now on. You have the microphone, and with it comes a responsibility to tell the truth.

The oceans are over-fished because of it. The amount of carbon is increasing because of it. The economy cannot provide for all of us because of it. 'It' is this: the earth is overpopulated relative to its resource base. Resources of soil, water and fossil fuels and minerals are limited, and we are exceeding their ability to support our needs. In the last 80 years, the Earth added five billion passengers to its life support systems in the last 80 or so years. Globally, the Earth continues to add 9,000 passengers each HOUR, net gain, each and every day to an already seriously overpopulated Earth relative to its limited resources. A good journalist would ask, "What resources can keep up with such an overwhelming demand?" and "How do we reduce carbon or our consumption of fish and other vital resources when we continue to grow our human numbers on an already overpopulated planet?"

Don't take my word for it. Do your homework. Look at all the evidence. For starters, check out the video interview with the late Dr. Al Bartlett, professor emeritus at University of Colorado Boulder at http://www.youtube.com/watch?v=F-QA2rkpBSY. I believe you will begin see that everything from pollution to traffic jams can be traced to the fact that well-fed people grow exponentially while our resources do not. We cannot have social justice until we address our overpopulation problem. I hope you do not fall into the trap of reporting that limiting family size is somehow worse than steering our planet away from catastrophe and collapse. Please don't forget to report that overpopulation is solvable by humanely reducing births with the intention to build a world that is truly sustainable.

You are our best hope for taking the lead on reporting fairly and frequently about our overpopulation crisis and our crucial need to humanely address it now.

Sincerely,

YOUR NAME HERE

Acknowledgements

Many thanks to World Population Balance, and its founder, president and overpopulation activist David Paxson. Thank you for helping me make the clearest possible argument about why most activists are on an unsustainable path. Thanks also to Alan Ware of World Population Balance for your excellent, thought-provoking edits.

Thanks to Dave Shea, the best editor and friend a person could have. Your polishing cloth must be worn out by now. Thanks for your humor and talents which add tremendously to my life.

Thanks to my husband John for understanding this issue so well and for your understanding and patience.

I dedicated my book to Ed Levering, an activist in the best sense of the word. He has dedicated his life to working on progressive issues of all kinds. His determination to incorporate the overpopulation issue into all of them is unique in the world. He is a passionate peace, justice and environmental activist. Ed deeply understands that all of his work outside of the overpopulation issue will not be successful if we do not focus on overpopulation as the crux of our problems. With a long list of protests under his belt, Ed never fails to try to place all of his humanitarian and wildlife-saving efforts under the umbrella of overpopulation. He follows in the footsteps of Martin Luther King Jr. who was able to work on multiple issues all at once. This book is dedicated to Ed's exemplary insight, passion and activism, and to our long-lasting friendship. May it be contagious to a world that needs your wisdom!

I also want to thank my fellow overpopulation activists. Some I have already met; others remain on the list of people I need to meet. You are my heroes. You encourage me every day to carry on despite obstacles both real and imagined.

My eternal gratitude to everyone at Freethought House for their courage and advice.

About the Author

Karen I. Shragg is a naturalist, writer and overpopulation activist. She joined the advisory board of World Population Balance in 2004, and regularly delivers lectures on overpopulation to local, state and national groups. Karen holds an Ed.D. from the University of St. Thomas in critical pedagogy and is director of the Wood Lake Nature Center in Richfield, Minnesota. Her other books include, *The Wolf Within: Poems to Awaken and Inspire in Times Like These*, *Grieving Outside the Box*, the *Nature's Yucky!* children's series with Lee Ann Landstrom, and *Lucy's Hero: Remembering Paul Wellstone*. She lives with her husband John in Bloomington, Minnesota.